John Gill:
Master of Rock

I would like to dedicate this book to Dave Rearick,
a remarkable climber and teacher.

John Gill:
Master of Rock
The life of a bouldering legend

PAT AMENT

Vertebrate Publishing, Sheffield
www.v-publishing.co.uk

John Gill: Master of Rock

Pat Ament

 Vertebrate Publishing
Omega Court, 352 Cemetery Road, Sheffield S11 8FT, United Kingdom
www.v-publishing.co.uk

First published in 1977 by Alpine House Publishing (Boulder, Colorado).
This edition first published in 2018 by Vertebrate Publishing.

Cover photo: © Matthew Coutts.

Images are reproduced by kind permission of Pat Ament.
Images © John Gill collection unless otherwise credited.

Pat Ament has asserted his rights under the Copyright, Designs and Patents
Act 1988 to be identified as the author of this work.

This book is a work of non-fiction based on the life, experiences and
recollections of Pat Ament and John Gill. In some limited cases the names
of people, places, dates and sequences or the detail of events have been
changed solely to protect the privacy of others. The author has stated to the
publishers that, except in such minor respects not affecting the substantial
accuracy of the work, the contents of the book are true.

A CIP catalogue record for this book is available from the British Library.

ISBN 978-1-912560-01-1 (Paperback)

ISBN 978-1-912560-00-4 (ebook)

Every effort has been made to obtain the necessary permissions with
reference to copyright material, both illustrative and quoted. We apologise
for any omissions in this respect and will be pleased to make the appropriate
acknowledgements in any future edition.

Produced by Vertebrate Publishing.

Printed and bound by Lightning Source Ltd.

Contents

Introduction

John Gill is the single most remarkable person I have come to know in the rock-climbing world. It is through a debt of gratitude to him that I have endeavoured to acquaint contemporary and future generations with his story. It is not my intent to define the man, nor to exploit his abilities, but rather to introduce his genius and independence of personality. His is a specialised kind of climbing – that of bouldering on reasonably small rock faces, of moving on almost impossible problems found within a few vertical or overhanging feet. Though known for bouldering, John climbed many longer routes, some roped and some solo, in the Needles of South Dakota for example, and put up lengthy first ascents in the Tetons in the later 1950s as difficult as anything in the country.

This book is divided into three sections. The first is a sort of essay on Gill: my particular view of him. I feel that I know Gill through rocks he and I have touched together. The second section consists of a series of impressions contributed by several outstanding climbers. The third part is a taped 'fireside chat,' an extensive interview in which Gill's opinions and experiences are drawn together in detail.

The activities of one of the heroes of mountaineering, the 'Don Quixotiade' of a boulderer, a subtle climbing innovator, may be interesting and fascinating not just to the devotees of the sport but to anyone respectful of the triumphs of a master.

Part 1

Essays on John Gill

1 The Thimble

In the early 1960s, my climbing partner, Fred Pfahler, told me about watching Gill perform in the Wyoming Tetons. I listened but was a sceptic, naturally. If I couldn't see those routes, then they were already out of mind, and so was Gill. Yet I was amused by Fred's exaggerations. My thoughts produced an agile climber hugging overhangs and pinching pebbles.

Prior to meeting Gill, I took a look at what was supposedly Gill's best route in the South Dakota Needles. Called The Thimble, the thirty-foot overhanging spire convinced me that Fred's hero was more than just some talented boulderer. Gill had transmuted into art a demon of desire; some kind of turning of the soul. Through the efforts of his imagination, Gill had found a line where one might never have otherwise existed. I stood searching for crystals and clues as to how it was to be done. Not only did the route appear to be harder than accomplished climbers would consider, but it was done ropeless directly above a guard railing.

Gill had left a tradition of excellence in the Needles, and The Thimble seemed to represent the degree to which he was able to surrender his inner self to climbing. This short journey upward, I could see, was a total and complete commitment. My earlier scepticism was partly based on rumours I had heard, putting Gill down as a 'mere boulderer.' Sceptics are of little consequence in the light of one very positive soul who pursues his personal goals, cognizant of but undisturbed by the views of others.

Gill demonstrated his technique and courage by way of The Thimble. There were levels which friends knew he could be depended upon to reach, yet he had surpassed such levels. It was a kind of awareness or philosophy which, I was beginning to see, characterised him, set him apart. He gave climbers in the Needles a glimpse of his reservoirs of determination, capturing in the inspiration of a moment the summit of a thimble-shaped spire.

It must have been something to behold if anyone was there to watch – Gill's strength and balance approaching their limits, hands tightening and feet edging ingeniously on fragile pebbles. Then, the elation or – who knows – depression, being at the top, knowing it was over; Gill in a world by himself contemplated the experience. He probably radiated a few sensations of pure joy or relief while at the highest point of that spire. Little was said by him about the route, before or after, for he did not brag. Climbers in the area the spring he did it were mystified and unable to do the route. They were unsure as to how to appraise the achievement.

As I stood below the Thimble, I no longer was a sceptic.

2 A Face in a Photograph

In 1964, Royal Robbins and I ambled underneath the various cracks and routes of a popular granite formation, Castle Rock, eleven miles west of Boulder, Colorado. Royal was looking for something to climb which had not been done before and was muttering something about John Gill. There were a couple of Gill routes on the rock, or so rumour had it.

We became interested in an imposing, twenty-foot-high bulge, and soon Robbins was hammering a piton into a crack, trying to get some protection. Was this one of the Gill routes? The landing was very rocky to attempt without a rope. After an effort and several mis-attempts, Royal and I succeeded at the climb and called it *The Final Exam*. We felt that we had done a respectable 'first.' I was in good shape, and Royal was recognised as one of the top two or three free climbers in America. In fact Gill had not done this route but, a year or so later during a visit to Colorado, would amble by and free solo our climb.

On another occasion, I discovered a preposterous finger-crack on a different side of the rock. This was one of the Gill routes, a friend, Mike Stults, assured me. The thing looked a lot like routes Mike had been told Gill did in Estes Park, Colorado.

All of this made it essential that I meet Gill, and I was happy to finally do so in 1968, at which time he confirmed that he had done that preposterous finger-crack. He also showed me a photograph of himself moving upward without a rope on *The Final Exam*. My big head began to shrink.

3　A Profiled Position

Six-foot-two, 180 pounds, and able to do a one-arm, one-finger pull-up, Gill is attracted to the more immediately gratifying or perhaps frustrating type of climbing which requires the use of such strength. West of Fort Collins, Colorado, is a series of short sandstone cliffs covered with routes he has done. These stand as monuments to him and will prove challenging, if not outrageous, to future generations of climbers. In 1968, Gill and I were climbing in this area and tested our abilities.

I watched him flow with exasperating ease up horrendous overhangs. The bouldering garden was illuminated by the finesse he employed while moving from hold to hold. My excruciating forays were comical, yet Gill was patient with me and helpful. He prodded me, and I was a sort of buffoon scratching a way upward. As I began a route of his, I was able to recall a letter I received in 1966. Royal Robbins had written the encouraging words, 'Sounds as if your strength and gymnastic ability are formidable. You should soon step into Gill's shoes as the boulder king of the U.S.' In an awkward position, I lunged for what I thought was a hold. In the twinkling of an eye, I returned – with amazing speed – to where I had started. I sat on the ground. Unspeakable pain penetrated my tailbone, and I had a rush of adrenaline – if not shock. Step into Gill's shoes? He picked me up.

For the remainder of the day, I enjoyed the role of observer. The failure had a redeeming quality, for I had awakened, seemingly, out of a daze generated by my conventional rock-climber's experience.

Through the beauty of his creations, Gill expressed his mentality. There was substance to Gill's climbing and to his quiet manner. With a refined outlook and carefully tempered hunger for perfection, he traversed, superbly balanced, into a profiled position. It was a sophisticated blend of insight and strength – muscle and technique in concert. A climbing world needs a John Gill to humble it … and to inspire it.

In 1968, at Split Rocks, an area located approximately halfway between Boulder and Estes Park, Colorado, Gill and I climbed the better part of a day. Jagged granite blocks strewn throughout the forest tore the flesh of our fingertips and shredded our egos. A warm sun made the day pleasant, and we discovered every sort of technique, every sort of problem. I was a little afraid to try a few of the routes which Gill ascended with authority.

When he spoke, it was as if his voice resonated in a deep cavity. Low and commanding, it was rarely heard except for a 'ho ho' in response to my whimpers. His silent nature was also a restless one, indicating the existence of a power which had been dormant too long.

He approached a smooth, overhanging, fifteen-foot wall and, at first, gently drew breath. Then his eyes became fixed upon a high hold. While compressing his upper torso, as if to recoil, he began to hyperventilate. To follow was a perfectly calculated slow-motion leap. There was a subtle, although important, shuffling of his feet on tiny nubbins. One hand reached over the rounded summit, the other pulled laterally. It was quick, and he hurled himself to the top of the boulder.

I squeezed the initial holds and sighed. I could grasp the holds but not the problem. After examining the fifteen-foot wall closely, it was, to me, the beauty and *savoir-faire* of Gill.

To be a disciple of his would be, I felt, an honour. I followed him about the boulders religiously and hoped he would bestow in me some fibre or hidden knowledge of the art. He tried to dispel my romantic notions with realistic talk of strength and technique insisted he had lots of weaknesses and that I was the real climber because I did longer routes and big-wall ascents.

We rigged a top rope, and Gill belayed me on a delicate wall. Initially, I was uncertain as to how to start. The only foothold was roughly the size of a pencil eraser. If I dislocated my shoulders, I could reach, for the left hand, a slippery pinch-edge and, for the right, a sickeningly small, sharp, fingertip flake. There was little advantage in knowing that John had climbed the route and judged it to be moderate! In his presence I found that I could push myself farther than I'd planned. I got a hand on the bucket-hold at the top before my weight went on to the rope. On a later visit to Split Rocks, I made the delicate wall and repeated it a number of times because it seemed to bring Gill to me when he was not there.

Upon discovering one of his tiny chalk arrows drawn on the rock near the bottom of certain deserving problems, a climber is able to intuit Gill's capacity for choosing an aesthetic line. These routes tend to be delicate and accurate, full of interesting nuances of character, and united by a theme.

I stood underneath one such route at Castle Rock, west of Boulder, Colorado, in 1969. Two small holds arrested the eye but were the only flaws in rounded, overhanging, bulging granite which arched out above a tiny, white arrow. I could tell I would have to search deep in order to see the solution to the moves. I wanted to see with Gill's eye. I approached the holds, prepared to follow a primitive urging of the blood and to scrapple a way upward, but was unable to find a sequence which worked. I was forced to resort to an extravagance of form, my right heel hooked on a tiny edge above my head, my hands crossed on a finger-crack and left foot frictioning on lichen. Talus below made me reluctant to extend myself, yet unlikely contortions and hard pulls brought me to a ledge and the end of the route. I was able to improve by identifying with Gill. I later would learn John's name for the route: *Acrobat Overhang*.

In 1969, I was sitting alone in a deserted Camp 4, the bouldering area of Yosemite. Pine needles were in my shoes, and chalk I had been rubbing on my fingers was in my hair. The boulders had worn me out after a couple hours of my climbing them. A breeze blew through the lofty trees, and I gazed upward at surrounding walls of granite which rose thousands of feet. A waterfall roared in the distance. The Sierra scene, spring smells, sun, and the sky were telling me to look beyond the surface of nature and separate myself from trifles. I was homesick for Colorado, yet persuaded to remain in Yosemite by some spell.

I began to reflect upon bouldering, its loneliness and frustration. In the hot afternoon, a drop of sweat in my palm became a crystalline image of John Gill. He was encouraging me to laugh at myself because I was too serious. In the little drop, I saw Gill caressing the underside of an overhang, climbing and clinging to it, then launching himself like an arrow upward toward some doubtful set of holds. I felt the intrigue of a man whose name was blowing softly through the forests of the Grand Tetons, the South Dakota Needles, Colorado, and many areas. I had visited Yosemite a number of times with increasing success on the boulders and realised that my new exertions were due, in part, to Gill. What I was doing on the boulders of Camp 4 was leaving a small mark, a few first ascents which would speak of what I had learned from someone whose skill was superior.

I wanted to be one with rock instead of at war with it. In the texture of the rock, I perceived ideals and drew upon the laugh in the Gill tableau. An odyssey filled me with a desire to climb hard but with a meticulous feel. I was charged with the electricity of Gill's touch. The reinforcement of his character transmitted to me from a distance. It became clear to me that so much of what Gill had taught the climbing world was only partly about climbing. I was drawn to contemplation, satisfied with lazily sitting, yet intoxicated to the point of elation with bouldering ideas and fantasies of the ridiculous. I wanted to nurture my perceptions, explore the boulders, know their value, and rise in the spirit of Gill above the wasteland of ego. In a momentary nostalgic feeling, a drop of sweat dissolved into callous.

After I returned to Colorado, I bouldered several times with Gill. On Flagstaff Mountain and in Eldorado Canyon, he did many of my best problems with ease. We visited some granite along the Gem Lake Trail near Estes Park and pushed our limits at Split Rocks. At Fort Collins, Gill came out to the cliffs with me but did not attempt to climb, because he had suffered a strain in his elbow. The injury was a nightmare to him, for the extent and seriousness of it were unknown, and it was accompanied by extreme pain, prohibiting him from doing even the simplest problems. We hiked to a forest with granite boulders west of Horse Tooth Reservoir where routes awaited exploration, and I pioneered a red, bulging wall which Gill gave to me since it would have been his. I was in my best physical and mental shape ever, and Gill, although depressed about his elbow, was inspired. The frustrations of his injury seemed to diminish with just the thought of climbing.

An evening on Flagstaff Mountain, overlooking the city of Boulder, Colorado, I climbed alone and was able to surpass some of my own goals on the coarse sandstone upon which I had worked for many years. I tested myself, moved as gracefully as possible, and felt complete composure. Gill's example was becoming a strong influence in my climbing and had begun to play a significant role in my development. Flagstaff was full of light and fall. I thought about Gill's injury and wondered if he was finished.

In the middle of winter, 1975, I bouldered with him in the badlands west of Pueblo, Colorado, and found he was far from incapacitated. Many climbers had thought he would never again reach his previous standard. He had recovered and, although acutely aware of the possibility of reinjury, climbed brilliantly. He showed me a route that he had found and achieved, a ferocious, twenty-foot, overhanging arête called *The Little Overhang*. This name was derived because the route was below another overhang at least twice as big. It scared me when John gave the upper overhang an inquisitive stare.

I was amazed that Gill could find a bouldering area near Pueblo. He had employed his sixth sense for discovering perfect little outcrops that just suited him. The routes were all difficult, and I was impressed enough to want to make a 16mm movie, a documentary of his form and style in bouldering. Gill had to be captured on speeding film. The first day of shooting, however, was a disaster. The camera I'd rented didn't work. It would run for about fourteen seconds, then stop. Gill was aware of the camera, especially when, at the crux move, it clicked off! It gave us a few laughs, if little footage. It was a bit disconcerting to Gill when, as he hung in the middle of a one-arm pull-up at the lip of an overhang, I snorted, 'The camera quit, can you hold it right there?'

In February 1976, I visited the Hagermeister boulders, near Estes Park, with a young climber of prodigious talent and originality, David Breashears. A cold wind kept us from climbing, so we simply toured the rocks, and I pointed out Gill routes. I saw in David's eyes an energy and clarity. He thought of bouldering someday with Gill. It seemed Gill's inspiration was to touch yet another generation; just by glancing at grey, lifeless rock, a respect for Gill could germinate.

I recalled visiting this place before ever meeting John, in days when the strength of the man was spoken of but rarely seen. I had searched out the area after hearing that a climber from the Needles had done several routes which would never be repeated. Some never have.

4   The Poetry of Mountaineering

Gill has been labelled a 'rock gymnast.' His movements are referred to as 'controlled dynamic technique.' Climbing magazines and alpine journals bear descriptive phrases such as, 'a supreme virtuoso in the fierce and concentrated difficulties of boulders and small rock faces' … One mountaineering publication observed that bouldering was 'an ascending order of excellence, determined purely by the degree of difficulty' … and such words are not quite wrong but not quite right.

Many competitive climbers view Gill as a fluke – merely a boulderer – a muscle man with little real courage, just a gymnast. Those unable to compete with Gill sometimes condescended to him and, although having never met him, have spoken of him as alien to popular climbing sensibility. Gill, however, has respected other types of climbers or mountaineers and been remarkably tolerant of their criticism. 'Too bad Gill doesn't do anything big,' a Yosemite climber said once, as if to belittle Gill or disparage bouldering. The comment seemed to imply that big-wall climbing was more significant than bouldering – a misconception, for they are separate arts, both valid, both demanding. Quantity does not imply quality. The difference between a boulder problem and an El Capitan route may be the difference between a poem by Yeats and a novel by Hemingway.

Bouldering is the poetry of mountaineering. It is climbing, distilled, and requires a different temperament, a different attention span. Climbers bemused or irritated by Gill (perhaps intimidated by his achievements or simply jealous) cannot seem to comprehend the rhyme or reason of such specialisation. As with good poetry, good bouldering comes from within. It is derived from an inner eye, then refined. Gill's activity on the boulders, the intensity of his climbing, and his precision.

In early May 1976, I bouldered with John on the buildings of the University of Southern Colorado, and then about twenty miles southeast of Pueblo, in a lost canyon. Again, I had the opportunity to watch and participate in the distillation. The day we bouldered on the buildings at the university Gill did routes involving long, fingertip hand-traverses. He clamped a large, square corner of concrete and ascend it. This defied any law of physics with which I was familiar. One route was a huge aerial swing from a sloping finger-ledge to the top of the building. He also had routes inside the buildings which he could do when the students were gone. He took me on a tour of the campus, and we wire-walked an occasional slack chain, pretending to cultivate balance but in reality, horsing around. It was a warm spring afternoon, and from campus we had a view of the eastern plain and the Rockies. This beauty of the day seemed to tranquillise us. John was silent and reflective as we ambled slowly back to the car.

The next day, it was a surprise when literally hundreds of great boulders appearing out of what seemed like a remote desert canyon. On either side of a sandy river in barren, cactus-covered country, Gill showed me overhangs and more overhangs. A gentle breeze blew through colourful foliage and cotton-wood trees along the banks of the river. The solitude was invigorating, and we happily succeeded or failed on any number of protruding, sandstone aretes. Steep yellow and brown faces kept us occupied for hours. Half the time, we simply imagined routes which might exist on boulders we saw at a distance. We seemed to be able to help each other in subtle ways and to motivate one another. I would discover a route, and John would climb it. Or John would climb a route, and I would discover that I could make it too. I did one route with balance, stemming, and footwork than John did by throwing himself with one arm up through the air. We laughed and basked in the hot sun as we struggled, in short bursts, upward.

John, while standing on the ground, was able to touch the lip of a large overhang. The only hold at the lip was a tiny, two-fingertip V-slot at which I scoffed. John wedged his two fingers, did a slow, one-arm pull-up, and reached a high hold.

On another side of the same rock, I formulated a static variation of a dynamic route which he had devised, and he gave me credit for doing it a 'better way.' It was a satisfying day and I felt close to Gill. Bouldering was not such fierce competition, but more a link between two friends; a link which perhaps is sometimes the essence of the poetry of mountaineering.

5   The Juggernaut

On Thanksgiving Day, 1976, I followed Gill back into the lost canyon south-east of Pueblo. We bouldered and spent a relaxing day in the sun. Dave Rearick was with us and occasionally wandered away from us to explore the exotic, silent cactus country or look for Indian petroglyphs. I spent most of the time film-ing, trying once more to get some footage of Gill on rock. The difficulty of filming John was that he preferred not to pose, so I had to work around him, frequently tripping over my tripod or having to crank the camera with Gill in the middle of a move.

A light wind blew across the land, over the strange, ruddy sandstone faces, softly stirring delicate leaves of cottonwoods. Cactus cloisters stood ominously almost everywhere, waiting for the right moment to reach out and grab some-one. We used a pair of climbing shoes to remove a clump of painful spears from John's leg.

During brief breaks from filming, I tried a few problems and managed to do the overhang with the fingertip V-slot John had shown me in the spring.

The canyon river was shallow, ice-encrusted, freezing brown slush which we had to wade with grimaces. Rearick expressed relief that the river was not a step wider, because he had no feeling below the knees.

After recovering, we watched Gill climb *The Juggernaut*. The idea of the route was to traverse a horizontal line of widely spaced fingertip holds along the lip of a large roof, and then go dynamically up an overhanging prow. Gill's feet hung in space, as he traversed out toward the prow. At one point he appeared to be in an iron cross on the rings. It was perhaps the most marvel-lous sequence of moves on a boulder that I had ever seen. Through the lens of the camera, Gill was perfect. He didn't need to be recognised as a climber or to receive notoriety for his skills. To be able to boulder was enough. The land-scape, the flat hills, the obscure dust-laden summits and small, rock-bottom pools sufficiently stimulated him. The breeze no longer blew, but the pungent fragrances of the desert flourished. Gill had found an area in harmony with his temperament. Gill reflected oneness, clutching the prow itself. He was bal-anced in an eerie lighting, in a cryptic, photogenic blur. He was aware of the brevity of life and fragility of experience. He climbed with a distinct love, a sil-houette on a horizon. In the late autumn afternoon, throughout the flowerlike desert beauty we shared Gill's magic grew.

Once at the top of *The Juggernaut,* he looked about at the endless scattered boulders and searched for more of them but was content with those he had found. Winter was not far off. His wife Dorothy was at home, cooking an elaborate dinner for us and expecting us to return soon. As we finished bouldering and walked to the car, Gill glanced back at the canyon, thinking that the new routes he saw would have to wait until spring. He stood overlooking the canyon on a precarious high rim of rock under a brilliant Thanksgiving sky, a climber transforming with his mind the ridiculous into sense.

6   Deliberating Poses

For John Gill, the art of bouldering is to increasingly refine the more aesthetic aspects of climbing – light, mood, atmosphere and difficulty. His approach has been inventive and free, and his progress towards mastery has drifted into climbing lore. He has climbed and bouldered in Georgia, Alabama, Illinois, Kentucky, New York, Wisconsin, Idaho, Montana, Wyoming, South Dakota, Missouri, Colorado, and Utah. Yet he has remained detached from the spectres of one-upmanship or glory seeking and has left in these areas ghostly charisma and mystical paths across rock.

Bob Kamps, author of *A Climber's Guide to the Needles in the Black Hills of South Dakota*, credits Gill with quite a number of first ascents, including the first free ascent of *The Javelin*, ascents of *Rook, Safety Pin, Duckpin, Pop Top, Pawn, Fin, Moby Dick, Leaning Tower, Falcon, Stumbling Block* (two routes), *Amorphous, Paydirt Pinnacle* (two very difficult routes), *Inner Outlet* (three difficult variations), *The Thimble* (two very difficult routes), *The Scab* (several problems), *Budweiser Spire, Wigwam, West Gruesome, Flying Buttress* (very severe), *Dusty Devil* (four routes), *Spike, El Mokana, the Incisor* (six routes), and *Do-Dad Spire*. The most impressive of these, the Thimble overhang, done by him in 1961 without any form of protection, was a magnificent achievement – as historically significant as any other 'ultimate' climb in the world. This twenty-foot overhanging wall had yet to be repeated at the time of publication of this book. Although unpublicised during the sixties, it may have been the quiet birth of some sort of metaphysics in bouldering. Kamps states that Gill 'reached a point where it seemed as safe to try for the summit as to retreat.' In the introduction to the guidebook, Kamps remarks: 'In the early '60s, John Gill put up a number of imposing routes on various spires, the most awesome being the north face of the Thimble. He attacked the boulders with singular devotion, and with strength sufficient to either pull himself up or pull the walls down. He moved in earnest against some of the many bulgy overhangs that abound and added to his already impressive accomplishments. One of his routes well worth pondering is the east face of the Outlet Boulder – dynamic force has surmounted a seemingly impossible bulge.'

At Blacktail Butte, in the Tetons, a number of very demanding climbs attest to Gill's poetry. His routes at Blacktail Butte have intimidated even the most competitive climbers. A few spry souls skylarking have bruised their knuckles attempting, with a top rope, to match wits with Gill, who, more often than not, free soloed. The Teton setting, the contour of the cliff, the exposure of the routes and difficulty of the moves, provide an unusual blend of beauty and challenge, and Gill's presence in the region will long be felt. For John, it was frequently a loner's game, exercising well above the landscape on an angular wall. Gill had no patronising air about him, no stiffness. He was simply able to manifest himself in deliberating poses on unsolvable, vertical stretches of rock. He did not 'conquer' that cliff, but rather drifted away subdued from the Jenny Lake Campground and drove toward Blacktail Butte with a desire to climb.

Gill is not an adolescent delusion. He is married and has two little girls. He is a gifted and prolific boulderer, a gymnast with the humour, mystery, and pathos of genius, a serious gentleman, a husband, a father, a professor of mathematics, an enigma yet also a real person able to suffer and to learn, a calm spirit with emotions and deep feeling. The devastating clarity of his view of climbing is more significant than his strength or ability. He has been an indirect mentor for several generations of bouldering specialists. He has likely accomplished the hardest moves anywhere in climbing, yet he has a reasonable view of such extremes. Many of his routes he wilfully contrives. For example, 'no-hand' routes have suited his fancy. Ascents of this type use little more than footwork, balance, and ingenuity, indicating that he is not just a show of strength and that he does not lack a sense for play. A couple of very competent climbers once were unable to repeat, with the use of all four of their limbs, one of Gill's no-hand fiascos. 'Eliminates,' as he calls them, are routes destined to be climbed rarely or even a single time.

Rich Goldstone, one of Gill's chief bouldering partners of the '60s, has mentioned that John did a number of 'eliminates' – bizarre and difficult problems – in the Shawangunks of New York. A handful of eastern climbers later tried everything from karate yells to shoulder stands with determined efforts to succeed. No one did.

Bouldering has been for Gill a kind of spiritual home. Loath to be restricted by climbing grades, he has invented a system of his own, whereby B-I, B-2, and B-3 vaguely signify the difficulty of routes. This classification has been as mysterious and misunderstood as the man himself. One can imagine a climber secure in the bliss and power of isolation.

Many climbers feel uncomfortable watching Gill boulder. It is uncanny and awkward to watch so much concentration. It may be slightly embarrassing to witness such superb control, or to observe the solitary work of a thinking brain. Listening to him hyperventilate at the start of a route is like listening to the warm-up of an Olympian.

Gill does not always climb. He is not obsessed. There are natural interludes in which he is unmotivated. He is attentive to his family and has been absorbed in his teaching profession and the rarefied atmosphere of abstract mathematical thought. When one gets to know him, it becomes obvious that he is a gentle person, and a humble one. He is a creature with a lot of decency whose character spills like cleansing light across shade and lichen, into the open pores of steep rock.

Climbers will ask: What are the faults which distinguish him? Does he have extraneous influences? What are his eccentricities? This must, necessarily, be a short admission, for there is little to be said about Gill's shy, defensive nature, or his occasional need to drink a beer and get mildly soused after a long day of teaching, or his playing the guitar and creating an original sound which lacks polish but is not without magnetism, or his undercooking French toast, or his peculiar constitution. He seems at times to enjoy depressing others with his routes, although this susceptibility – almost perverse desire – is seldom revealed. Some of these character traits are, at most, the result of his detachment, or of an inclination to be under the spell of internal adventures.

Part 2

Whispers of a Legend

Following are several short personal impressions of Gill contributed by notable climbers.

7 A Pair of Long Legs by Dave Rearick

In August 1960, I spent two or three weeks in the Tetons, at the climbers' campground on the south shore of Jenny Lake, which the rangers had created a year or two earlier to try to keep the climbing scene out of the sight of the general public. There's no trace of that campground anymore, except maybe the old kilns that Yvon Chouinard and Ken Weeks were sleeping in; or the big tree in the clearing where one night somebody, likely the Vulgarians, lassoed a bear and pulled him down with a rope attached to a truck; and perhaps the large cement slab of unknown origin is still there, on which, for several hours every morning, John Gill and I practised our hand balancing. John was able to do a 'stiff-stiff' body press, and I kept working on it, getting a little closer every day with encouragement from John, but never quite succeeding until finally, right after he left and there was no one to show off for, I did five of them in a row. For lunch we'd go over to the little general store run by two old ladies and try to absorb as much protein as possible. John favoured a thick, pasty mixture of powdered milk as a good muscle-builder, never mind what it tasted like. In the afternoons, we had long sessions of hatchet throwing, along with Bill Woodruff who had bicycled across from Yosemite and was resting up before riding further east. Later on, John would usually drive over to Blacktail Butte for an hour or two of solo climbing. I never accompanied him there, and few people knew just what he was up to, but Bob Kamps went along once or twice and later told me he couldn't top-rope some of the things John was soloing. As for the little boulders around the campground, there was not one, even if only knee-high, that had not felt the tread of John's tightly laced climbing shoes on whatever tiny crystals or minute features it offered by way of a bouldering problem.

John Gill was a frequent visitor at the Jenny Lake Ranger Station, usually not to sign out for a climb but to practice fingertip front levers on the doorjamb. From the parking lot, all you could see was a pair of long legs extending horizontally out the front door, knees together and toes carefully pointed. All of his exercises, from his most outrageous bouldering manoeuvres down to his frisbee throwing with garbage can lids, were executed with the utmost control and painstaking attention to style; and all of this, together with his agreeable manner and a certain intriguing reluctance to separate reality from absurdity, made John an outstanding companion for whiling away those long, exuberant summer days.

8   That Morning by Paul Mayrose

This is a tale of a first encounter – stereotyped perhaps, but quite real nevertheless – with John Gill. Bouldering was a new concept around Estes Park, Colorado, in the early 1960s. None of us locals were quite sure how to approach it. It could be entertaining, but should it ever be taken seriously? The answer put in an appearance one pleasant Saturday afternoon.

It was the Hagermeister boulders. I don't remember the cast of characters. Bob Bradley was certainly there, Dave Rearick almost certainly ... and perhaps half a dozen others. A familiar face arrived, accompanied by a person who was introduced as John Gill. Mr Gill was a tall person, quiet, and not particularly impressive physically as long as he stood absolutely still! If he moved in the slightest, he rippled and bulged. I decided that he was healthy.

As the afternoon progressed, so did most of us. Ah, the competitive instinct! Gill got quite far enough off the ground to convince me that bouldering was not any kind of sop for frustrated acrophobiacs. His funny business enabled the rest of us to climb better without getting overly philosophical.

He climbed, and I watched. He climbed, and we fell off in his wake ... in droves. Eventually, I became convinced that he wasn't actually strong enough to cheat by gouging his own holds into the rock. A few of the cast became discouraged and left. I, and others, got mad and determined and stayed and started getting up occasional things we would not have recognised as climbable that morning.

Bouldering had come to Estes Park in earnest. Basic concepts hadn't been changed, but the order of magnitude certainly had. I took up bouldering. For me it was never an end in itself, but it became the difference between 5.8 and 5.9 (even a little 5.10) on bigger climbs. As always, advance stemmed from one individual who pushed beyond convention. A committee of 5.8 climbers cannot meet and climb 5.10 or anything but 5.8. But, one man can: John Gill showed me that levels of climbing could be pushed higher. Knowing him, I went in search of my own limit. Apparently I found it, but I have never since tried to guess the upper bounds for someone else. Not bloody well likely after the shock of a first meeting with Gill.

9 Zen and the Art of Rock Climbing
A tape-recorded statement
by Yvon Chouinard

I don't remember when I met Gill. It must have been the late '50s. There were few climbers in the Tetons in those days, mainly people from the eastern colleges, Dartmouth, Harvard … Climbers on their way to expeditions in Alaska or somewhere would stop through the Tetons. A handful of people were intensively climbing in the Tetons and lived there the whole summer, scrounging on fifty cents a day, eating oatmeal. At that time, Gill was doing some climbs on Disappointment Peak. After grabbing whatever climbing partner he could find, he'd do some little arête that often wouldn't lead anywhere because Disappointment Peak is just a big flat thing on top. Kamps and I did Satisfaction Buttress, and it was the hardest climb in the Tetons when we did it, yet the *American Alpine Journal* refused to publish anything about it because it didn't have a summit. That was where climbing was, in those days. If it didn't have a summit, you really didn't do a climb. Gill was getting even more ridiculous and was doing things just for the sake of pure climbing, going nowhere. These were absurd climbs, as far as the Alpine Club was concerned. Now people do a one-pitch climb, and it's a route, so I guess he was ahead of his time in that respect. He wandered about looking for the hardest routes; when a party would go to repeat a route Gill had given a 5.8 or 5.9 rating they would find it to be 5.5, because Gill had done some unlikely variation which they could not discover. He wouldn't do the most logical way. He'd go out and enjoy himself on hard problems.

I did a couple routes with him on … The Knob? These were several-pitch, roped climbs. At that time, he was a smooth climber, always under control, but he didn't seem to be a bold climber. There are some people who are extremely bold who aren't exceptional physical climbers, but boldness gets them up the climb. Maybe Gill didn't need to be bold then. He used to do a lot of roped leads, although I don't think he ever really cared for it. He enjoyed bouldering much more and, I believe, was happier when he realised that. There were a few people soloing or specialising, but climbing with a rope and a partner was, for the majority of people, what it was all about. He didn't excel at that particular part of it. It may have tended to make him a bit insecure that everyone else was climbing with a rope. He chose to specialise in one form of climbing, pure bouldering, and specifically, overhanging face climbing. He loved overhangs. He never really got into crack climbing. There was little crack climbing in the country except for around Boulder and in Yosemite until recently, and you didn't have an opportunity to do much of it on boulders unless you wanted to go to out-of-the-way areas.

Gill and I developed some of the climbs on the boulders in the Tetons. I don't think there were any routes there before we started. We named the boulders and worked on them for hours at a time. *Falling Ant Slab* was named because the angle was such that ants would go up, reach a point, and peel off! On Red Cross Rock, there was a route called *Cut-Finger* where you had to use a hold that would ... cut your finger. There were sharp quartz crystals, and you'd come back from a day of bouldering with your hands in shreds. That's why we called the boulder Red Cross Rock. On *Falling Ant Slab,* we would do climbs no-hands, or one-hand, trying out all different problems. Gill had a couple of really exceptional climbs. In those days, I could do many of the climbs, but three or four I didn't have a chance with. He had well over a foot reach on me. The only thing I used to get him on were occasional no-hand routes. I had a much lower centre of gravity. But, when I first bouldered with Gill he was nowhere as good as a few years later. He was getting better very fast.

We wrote a little guidebook to the Jenny Lake boulders. Gill did the drawings for it and the gradings of the routes. I wrote the text. I think it's still available. It's a classic. The rangers have the one copy and guard it. We wrote it tongue in cheek and patterned it after the guide to the Tetons which says, 'These mountains are big mountains, they make their own weather.' We wrote the same about the boulders: 'These are big boulders, they make their own weather.' We talked about the north faces and the big south faces.

We'd boulder just about every day. We'd take visiting climbers to the boulders on rainy days and show them the routes. Gill and I shared the same campsites for years and would go together to Blacktail Butte. Blacktail Butte is grey limestone, absolutely ninety degrees, all finger holds. I remember the third route he did there. I'm sure it's 5.10. It may have been one of the first 5.10s in the country, because that was about 1959 or so. It's one of those things where you've got to go quickly and you've got to conserve strength. Your forearms get pumped up. Of course, he didn't have to go very fast, because his arms never gave out.

It's amazing that Gill has bouldered for so long. Maybe it's one of the reasons he's so good. He's been at it for twenty years. He hasn't gone on to other types of climbing. He has stayed with it. He's an exceptional athlete anyway.

Right now, climbing is still in a stage of pure physical movement, and the next step is going to be mind control. I think Gill has already gone into that, from watching him prepare for a boulder even in the late '50s. I would walk up to a boulder and just do it. He would sit below a route, do his little breathing exercises, and get his mind prepared, like a weight lifter walking up to a set of weights, getting his mind calmed down and his body ready to go. You're going to have to use meditation and yoga to be able to get up some of the new climbs, because pure physical strength or technique are not going to be enough. You're going to have to climb as if you're two feet off the ground. I think it's going to be Zen and the art of rock climbing. It's happening in a lot of areas, such as tennis. That's what the book *The Inner Game of Tennis* is all about. They've taken people who are learning tennis, and one group goes out and plays every day for two weeks while another group just sits down, meditates, thinks about improving, thinks about how they're going to swing the racket, getting it all set in their minds, and the group that concentrates on it rather than plays becomes more skilful. Climbing is going to be the same way. You know, you can go out one day and play pool, and you're just an average player, but you simply look at the balls and know they're going to sink in the pockets. You grab the cue, you don't even think, then you run the whole table. You try to do it another day, and you can't. Why does that happen? When it gets to the point where we can, at will, conjure up these exceptional days, there'll be some incredible things occurring. It'll happen on the boulders before it happens in other areas of climbing.

10 A Visit to Red Cross Rock by Jim Erickson

In 1963, I am a beginning climber at Devil's Lake, Wisconsin, and experienced climbers tell engrossing stories around the campfires. The name John Gill is attached to tales of a person able to do one-arm pull-ups while pinching the 2 × 4s of a basement ceiling. Gill seems to possess more of the qualities of heroic myth than of flesh and blood. Yet, climbs at Devil's Lake are there to prove the myths: *Gill's Corner, Gill's Crack, Sometime Crack, the Flatiron* …

In August 1964, my brother and I are in the Tetons contemplating the underside of Red Cross Rock, a twelve-or-so-foot, mushroom-shaped boulder. Two figures wander over to us, and we recognise Rich Goldstone whom we know from Devil's Lake. We exchange greetings, and Rich introduces us to his companion, John Gill. Dave and I nearly faint, for we've half believed that Gill had no corporal existence. We observe, as the two climbers use mysterious white chemicals on their fingers, mats for their feet, and tiny lichen brushes while devising extreme routes up the boulder.

Finally, Gill moves to the north corner overhang, stands on a small foothold, grabs an undercling with his left hand, and reaches with the other hand out over the bulge for what appears to be nothing. He simultaneously springs and does a one-arm, fingertip pull-up on this nothing. Dave and I fail to comprehend what we have seen and, after the two leave, examine that hold. It is about an eighth of an inch wide.

11   Credence by Steve Wunsch

Ever wanted to make an outrageous assertion and get away with it? Just pick the blankest side of a boulder or the most ridiculous looking overhang and say that a few years ago you saw John Gill walk by and climb it. Now if the individual you are trying to 'sandbag' has had the privilege of visiting areas where Gill has climbed, the worst you're likely to meet in the way of scepticism is a wide-eyed 'How?'

Kevin Bein was disarmingly well prepared for my query ('How?') and responded with a flourishing, carriage-road ballet amply narrated with talk of side-pulls, levers, and swing moves. He almost had me believing it until he had Gill jumping off from several feet above the overhang where Gill thought better of trying to mantel on a pile of sloping wet leaves.

'Nobody would jump off from up there!' I said.

'He did. He downclimbed a move first, jumped off, then walked on down to the next problem.'

Well, sandbagging is the name of the game in the Shawangunks, so, while we were setting up the top rope, I half-sensed that I was about to be taken for a ride, and I don't mean up. This supposed climb sported an overhang just as big and about as high as *Doug's Roof* (indeed it was the same roof but went over just a bit left, where there was no crack). The number of man-hours and roped falls which went into the freeing of *Doug's Roof* are an embarrassing matter of public record. If Kevin had tried this tale on me using anyone but Gill as its hero I'm sure I would have dismissed it instantly. But, the mere mention of Gill's name evokes memories that seem to establish credence for the wildest of human aspirations. Didn't I try every Sunday one winter to do the left side of the *Eliminator* at Fort Collins? I eventually got the lunge on that climb down well enough to bloody my left hand consistently on the hold, but not hang on to it. I've seen pictures of him doing it without a rope. Or being in the Needle's Eye parking lot digging into my pack for the compass (I never did need it on Ben Nevis) to see if that really was the Thimble's north face. It was. Or standing under the *Red Cross Overhang* in the Tetons after years of trying, listening to the drizzle in the forest (I'd never really gotten high enough for rain to matter), thinking of the first bouldering I did in the Tetons, years before, and a bright-eyed young friend saying with awe, almost whispering, 'Want to see a 5.13 climb?' I did.

All modesty aside, I began to realise that this overhang with the rope now dangling down past it might actually go, unbelievable as it had seemed only minutes before. I even fancied that, using slight modifications of Kevin's pantomime, I might do it. However, it seems I had made some miscalculations as to the sizes of, and distances between, each of the holds and was quickly swinging on to the rope, glad at least of my calculation that 'nobody would jump off from up there.' In fact, I didn't get anywhere near the spot Gill jumped off from; nor, to my satisfaction, did anyone else that day.

12 Miscellaneous Interchange
Obtained from write-ups, letters, phone calls, and first-hand discussions

'On the way to one of Gill's bouldering sites, I see that more than the mere physical effort of climbing is required. It takes a gift to actually locate these areas. Observing Gill in profile driving his Volkswagen bus, I imagine his fingers being, in actuality, witching sticks for locating boulders. Gill, Ament, and I arrive at an amphitheatre of rock where the opera is to begin. John's dog, a red, half-Irish Setter named Gallo, scruffles up the backside of the amphitheatre and races along the rim of the cliffs, then finds a pool of mud and water in which to play. Standing at the base of the Ripper Traverse, Gill breathes in gasps. He does not touch the rock, nor does he simply climb it. He, in essence, transcends the route. He is across it.'   – Bob Candelaria

'Gill is the true spiritual climber from whom we can all learn.'
– David Breashears

'So strong and directed is Gill's presence. He is a performing artist, a hero in an age of anti-heroes, a model for all who aspire to achievement. Last night I had dreams about Gill. He climbed in different spaces of time, and the spaces were called zones. Gill could perceive the zones, but they were not within my grasp!'
– Tom Higgins

'In the Needles in the '60s, I found Gill to be a little aloof or cold. But, I can only recall bits and pieces. I remember that Royal tried unsuccessfully to duplicate Gill's feat on the Thimble. There was a short, leaning face which Gill was able to climb by starting atop a small, round piece of wood. With this cheater's stick, he was able to reach the first holds of the route, but he wouldn't allow me the use of a ten-foot log to stand on.'
– Bob Kamps

'Gill jumped off from about twenty feet up and landed like a cat in the midst of jagged talus boulders.'

– Rich Goldstone

'A walk through the Needles would be a relaxing joy suddenly shattered when one of our troupe would spy a tiny white arrow pointing up an overhanging bulge or smooth slab. The idea that they were drawn in jest faded as we learned more about Gill. We made an ascent of the Thimble's easy side. The summit register said, 'Hats off to John Gill,' signed by Royal Robbins. Gill had done the overhanging side of the rock, to Royal's and everyone's amazement. A trip to the Spire 1 area gave us our first glimpse of Gill. He was high up, alone on the spire. It was the first solo ascent of the route. Renn Fenton showed us a boulder problem, a smooth, flared, upside-down trough with an arrow, and said that even when Gill strained you didn't know it.'

– Paul Piana

Part 3

An Extensive Interview with John Gill

13 A Chat with John Gill
January 1976

After a spaghetti dinner and some wine, John Gill and I sat at the kitchen table in his large, two-story house in Pueblo, Colorado. We talked climbing for a couple of hours with a cassette tape recorder running, then retired to the living room and continued the discussion until the recorder shut off. It was not so much an interview as just talk. After a while, the language became uninhibited, we forgot about grammar, and we laughed. Some of our comments later seemed downright spaghetti-bloated!

It felt good to hear Gill tell the stories – many of which had reached the climbing world in one or another distorted form. John's words are important and will be instructive and applicable to mountaineers, big-wall climbers, and boulderers alike. He spoke slowly and methodically.

At times, he dismisses the legends. Gill takes us on a journey which is only a step from being perceptible by touch:

> **Ament:** *When did you start climbing? How did you get an interest in it?*
> **Gill:** In 1953, I had a girlfriend in high school who had some experience climbing in Colorado and Wyoming. I believe she had even taken a trip to Europe.
> **Ament:** *She took you up?*
> **Gill:** Yes, a group of several of us visited north Georgia on a number of occasions during 1953, and the mountains of northern Georgia are low hills, really, compared to the peaks out here. But, there were some nice limestone and sandstone outcrops, and we did some easy climbing. That's the way I got introduced to it. We just had a lot of fun. We didn't push ourselves. I wore floppy basketball shoes.
> **Ament:** *Were you already into gymnastics at this time?*
> **Gill:** Not yet.
> **Ament:** *Did you get interested in gymnastics and rope climbing through rock climbing?*
> **Gill:** Yes, I definitely did.
> **Ament:** *Rumour was that you were a rope climber and gymnast and that you just happened to notice climbing and got on the rock and were good.*

Gill: It's actually the reverse. I did not engage in any form of organised athletics in high school. But, we started going up to north Georgia and doing some easy rock climbing at places such as Stone Mountain, right outside of Atlanta. I was living in Atlanta at the time. During the summer of 1954, a friend, Dick Wimer, and I drove out in his old car to Colorado and did a number of climbs. We spent most of the month of August in Colorado. I recall climbing the regular route on the Maiden, having a lot of fun on that. We did some mountain hiking, more of that than actual rock climbing. We did Longs Peak. I soloed a route on the East Face of Longs – a fairly easy route.

Ament: *How old were you?*

Gill: Sixteen. But, it was an easy route. The lower portion of it was on the buttress below which the glacier is situated. I recall crossing the glacier at one point and getting on to Broadway (the ledge system which runs across the East Face of Longs at mid-height). There I was joined by a guide – can't recall his name right now, or who he was working for ... Whatever the guide service was at that time. Al ... Hays, I believe. In any event, he had seen me scrambling around up there and, I guess, thought I was a tourist idiot and came wandering up to see what I was doing. We had a little discussion on Mills Glacier, and he became convinced that I wasn't a complete idiot. So, we decided to go on to the top. He had come up that day actually to replace the summit register, and I had stumbled over a route that he had anticipated doing himself. I had a short length of rope with me, a little piece of nylon about fifty feet long. We roped together and did the upper portion of the face, on through the little notch. It was a lot of fun. I do recall that he had a very painful journey coming back, because he had a trick knee, and it went out ... I don't believe on the summit, but down in the boulder field. He hobbled all the way back, with a couple of ice axes.

Ament: *You were just visiting Colorado that trip and went back to Georgia?*

Gill: Right. Then I enrolled in Georgia Tech that fall, and they had a good gymnastics program. But, actually, that wasn't what got me started in gymnastics so much as the fact that every freshman had to take three physical education activity courses, one each quarter. And one of these was gymnastics. Another was swimming. The third was track and field. I think I took the track and field first and was unhappy with that. But, when I got into gymnastics, I discovered that I had really found an athletic home that I hadn't anticipated. I had a good time in the course. Later, I worked out with the Georgia Tech gym team for about a year.

Ament: *What was your apparatus?*

Gill: I started on rope climbing, which was a legitimate event at the time. I could climb rope quite well the first day I walked into the gymnasium, although I'd really never done any of that sort of thing before, apart from the kind of arm exercise you get doing fairly simple rock climbing. I surprised myself. I discovered that I could zip right up there. That was my primary apparatus. Then I did some work on my own on the parallel bars, a little bit on the high bar. The rings always fascinated me. I was too weak then to do anything hard on rings, but started working on preliminary moves. I left Georgia Tech after two years and transferred to the University of Georgia, and there was no gymnastics team, so from that point on I worked out on my own. I started working the still rings more, I suppose, than any other apparatus. I climbed the rope fairly frequently but just didn't have the enthusiasm for it that I'd had at Tech. However, the rings continued to fascinate me, and I built up a fair amount of strength. When I entered Georgia Tech, I weighed about 140 pounds. By the time I graduated from college, I was up to about 185, maybe 190. There wasn't much fat on that.

Ament: *Was the build-up from rope climbing mostly or from rings?*

Gill: The rope didn't actually develop much muscle. I could climb rope fairly well when I first started. Of course, I didn't develop refined rope climbing technique until I had practiced for several months. I climbed rope on and off with the team for a while, and that's really the only competitive event I engaged in.

Ament: *How far did you go with the competition?*

Gill: Just local. I dropped off the team after a short time. I was never really all that good at gymnastics. Although I was fairly good at rope climbing, my body was just a little too long, and I was too inflexible to be really good on other apparatus.

Ament: *Were you continuing rock climbing right along with gymnastics?*

Gill: Yes. I suppose I really started bouldering – and, by that, I mean climbing short difficult things – in 1955 or 1956. Difficult in those days meant 5.7. I was enthusiastic about gymnastics – not so much from the standpoint of it being an excellent sport as from the fact that it contributed to climbing. And I was pretty interested in climbing at the time.

Ament: *Then you graduated from the University of Georgia?*

Gill: Yes. I went into the Air Force. I had been in the R.O.T.C. program at the University of Georgia and so got a commission. I went in as a meteorology officer. The following year, 1959, the Air Force sent me to the University of Chicago to study meteorology for a year. I was happy to be reasonably close to Devil's Lake, Wisconsin. I had visited the area once before, on a trip with my parents in the early '50s. I climbed there that fall (1959), probably seven or eight times.

Ament: *How close was this from where you were stationed?*

Gill: Technically, I was stationed at the University of Chicago. But I was completely independent of the Air Force at that point, other than going to classes, you know, doing my work, picking up my pay cheque. We didn't have to wear a uniform, and I had my weekends free. The college vacations were time we could take to do what we wished. It was mostly on weekends that I visited Devil's Lake. It was not a long drive. I also enjoyed working out in the gymnasium with the University of Chicago gymnastics team. I met several talented performers there and developed some skills. When I graduated from meteorology training at Chicago, I was assigned to Glasgow Air Force Base in Montana. That's when I moved out west. The base was located in the north-eastern corner of Montana, very remote, well away from all the big mountains. It's not one of the prettier spots in Montana.

Ament: *Hearsay had it that you worked out alone in some tower while studying the clouds.*

Gill: As a weather forecaster, sometimes things would get a little dull, say on an evening shift, and I would go up into the control tower and do chin-ups, things like that, to pass the time. But, there was a good base gymnasium, and I kept up my gymnastics. By this time, I had purchased a rope and also had a set of rings. As soon as I arrived in Montana, I hung these up in the base gymnasium. In some of my spare time, I would go over and work out, usually every other day for one to two hours. Originally, I had been assigned to Montana for a period of two years. But, my tour of duty was extended during the Berlin crisis, so I stayed two years, eight months. When I left the base in May 1962, I packed my Volkswagen full of all sorts of goodies, shipped my major belongings to my parents' house in Alabama, and took off to spend most of the summer traveling, bouldering, hiking, having a good time for a change. I started off by driving all the way down to Zion and doing some hiking and bouldering there. Then I visited various places in Colorado. I remember meeting Dave Rearick. I had met him the first time in the Tetons in 1957 or 1958. I believe, in that summer of 1962, he was a ranger at Longs Peak. I went back to Alabama that fall. I wanted to get a master's degree in math. So, I was in Alabama for two years, from 1962 to 1964, during which time I again did gymnastics on my own. I went bouldering in northern Alabama. There were even some places around Tuscaloosa (where I was born) and Birmingham with solid sandstone outcrops that were fun to climb on. So I kept up my climbing skill there. I'm not sure it improved, but at least it didn't regress all that much. After I received my master's degree, I got a job as an instructor at Murray State University in Kentucky, about two hundred miles north of Tuscaloosa. I moved up there and spent three years in the Mathematics Department, three very pleasant years. During that time, I was conscientious about gymnastics. I had several Persian friends, students at Murray State, who taught me how to play soccer. I found excellent places to do short rock climbing, or bouldering, in southern Illinois – Dixon Springs, for example. That was where I went most frequently. Pennirile Forest State Park in Kentucky was another area that I visited once or twice. That's where the sequence was shot that we were looking at today where there's a dynamic move up to a ledge, then the hand traverse out … I had a lot of fun climbing on weekends at Dixon Springs. Some friends, Rich Goldstone, Bob Williams from Northwestern, Ray Shragg, all from the Chicago area, came down two or three times during that period, visited me, and climbed at the Springs. Cave-In Rock State Park, on the Ohio River, was another area. That was primarily limestone. At the end of three years, I really felt that if I wanted to progress professionally I'd have to acquire a PhD. So I looked around and tried to find a school which was reasonably good at the doctoral level of mathematics. It didn't have to be Yale or Harvard, but a reasonably good school that was near a very nice area with good boulders, hiking, swimming, fishing, and all the rest. I toyed with the idea of going to Colorado University but got a better offer as a graduate teaching assistant at Colorado State University. I stayed at C.S.U. just as long as I possibly could, nearly four years. I climbed at Horse Tooth Reservoir frequently. During good weather, I would go out, on the average, every other day for a couple of hours. It didn't amount to much driving. A trip of about ten minutes and you'd be there. I met Rich Borgman, because I went over to the campus gymnasium and got into a conversation with the gymnastics coach. When he learned that I was a climber, he mentioned that there was a member of the gymnastics team who, quote, 'could crawl all over the walls without any visible holds.' Naturally this piqued my curiosity! I looked Rich up, introduced myself, and we became very good friends. We spent hours at the lake, quite a bit of the time merely exploring, finding new boulders.

Ament: *It turned out to be true that Rich could climb around with no visible holds.*

Gill: Yes, unfortunately.

Ament: *You couldn't have found a better partner.*

Gill: Well, then of course I met you during that time. And I met several other people. I started seeing a lot of very good boulderers.

Ament: *Before we progress into more recent events, could we go more into your climbing in the Needles?*

Gill: The first time I visited the Needles was on a trip west with my parents in 1955. We drove through the Black Hills. I recall jumping out of the car, running over and climbing some little spire which was probably 3rd class but seemed pretty scary at the time. My second visit was in September 1957. I used to spend a lot of my summer time climbing and hiking around the Tetons. And, at the end of a stay there, a friend and I drove over and spent a couple of weeks in the Needles. I really became engrossed in them. I saw the possibilities. It would be unfair to say that little had been accomplished up to that point. Quite a lot had been done. The legendary climbing team of Herb and Jan Conn had climbed a tremendous number of individual spires. I recall that we were very impressed that summer with the routes they had done. We repeated some of their better routes. For example, the South Tower at that time was considered to be one of the most difficult routes. It's 5.7 or 5.8. And it was a little scary then. I didn't have the right size piton when I went up there and was wearing some degenerate, floppy climbing shoes that kept curling up on edge holds and slipping off. So it was more exciting than perhaps it should have been. That fall (1957) I really became very interested in the Needles and decided to come back as frequently as possible. When stationed at Glasgow I would visit the Needles occasionally, and it was eventually on one of these extended weekend trips that I did the Thimble overhang, the second overhanging route on the spire. In order to establish a parking lot at the Needle's Eye, a tiny bit of the Thimble had been chopped away, at the base of the overhang. It's the logical place to park your car if you want to do any climbing in that area. Each time I'd come back to the car, I'd look around, you know, and see if there was anything that seemed interesting to play on. There are plenty of climbs you can see from the parking lot that other people have done. I had put up a route in 1960 with Bill Woodruff that followed a sort of groove or slot on the left side of the actual overhanging face of the Thimble.[1] And I hadn't thought too much more about it. But one day, coming back from climbing, I looked up at this overhanging wall and saw that there was a possible route to the right of the little slot – but barely possible. It's hard to say what caused me to become so attached to it. I suppose it was a psychological point in my climbing career, and I felt as though I had to really produce, really do something substantial. I hadn't done all that much yet. My forte was short climbs. I wasn't interested in the longer climbs. At this time, the longer climbs, and, of course, I mean the more impressive ones, were the bolt ladders, the chains of pitons, and so on, things in Yosemite. That didn't appeal to me. I couldn't get to those areas anyhow. But, this thing appealed to me. It was aesthetic and very clean. There were very few holds on it. I was a lot less concerned with safety in those days than I am now. Nowadays I'll put a rope on to cross the street or to step off the curb. Maybe not to cross the street, but certainly to step off the curb! But, that was a psychological high point in my climbing career. I felt as though I had to do something with an element of risk in it, something difficult. This particular tentative climb seemed to combine those characteristics just beautifully, maybe even too much so. I looked it over very carefully, scrambled halfway up the route on the left and looked at the holds. I saw what sorts of moves I would be responsible for, if I were willing to commit myself to the climb. At this time, I was stationed in Montana. So I went back to the base and started to devise ways, around the gym, in which to train for some of the difficult moves that I would have to do on the Thimble. I did all sorts of peculiar things that made a lot of people working out in the gym hysterical. There were a couple of long reaches on the Thimble, and of course you're on your

---

1 This route itself is a very serious lead – Editor.

fingertips practically the whole way. There's a hold about half-way up that separates the climb into two psychological parts. You have to go off of it quite a way. I did squeeze-type exercises, because I noticed that there were some little nubbins up there that I would have to squeeze when the horizontal holds ran out. They run out pretty fast. I devised little climbs on nuts and bolts sticking out of the wall of the gymnasium. I would squeeze the bolts and pull myself up. When I was at the University of Chicago, I had developed the ability to do a one-arm pull-up on the first joint of my fingers. I really needed this ability – both from the standpoint of sheer power for single moves and of stamina for hanging on some small hold for a long period. I did a lot of doorjamb chin-ups with two hands and got to the point where I could do possibly three in a row on one arm on my fingertips. I was also doing regular one-arm pull-ups and got to about seven of those with my right arm and five or six with my left. I trained for a period of one winter. The Thimble was on my mind during that whole time. The following spring, I visited the Needles. I forget whether it was on the first or second trip down, but I did eventually get up the route. It wasn't all that much fun.

Ament: *The guard railing below you must give you incentive.*

Gill: If you fall completely out of control, you do run the risk of hitting that. What I did was climb up and down the bottom portion of the route on a number of different occasions, getting to about midpoint. I had that much completely wired. I was climbing down but could jump off also. I jumped off once or twice. Probably the reason I have a little back trouble, foot trouble, and toe trouble right now is that I jumped off of boulders frequently in my younger days. But, I had the bottom portion of this climb wired before I committed myself to the top and it was just a process of going up and down, up and down. Eventually, I worked myself into such a fevered pitch that I committed myself to the top portion and very fortunately made it. It's like a lot of other sporting activities. You not only get psyched up but almost become hypnotised or mesmerised to the point where your mind goes blank, and you climb by well-cultivated instinct. You do it.

Ament: *Was it your hardest climb?*

Gill: Well, it was sure the scariest. I don't know that the individual moves are the hardest that I have made. I doubt that seriously. I think I have made harder moves, but not over such an extended expanse of rock, and not under such desperate circumstances. It takes a lot of stamina and a substantial, though somewhat foolish, commitment to climb it.

Ament: *Was this done before your hard bouldering in the Tetons or afterwards?*

Gill: It was about the same time, I think. It seems to me I climbed that one route on Red Cross Rock, the difficult centre overhang, in about 1959 or 1960, maybe a year before I did the Thimble route.

Ament: *Could you relate some of the climbing you did in the Tetons other than bouldering? There is hearsay that you did desperate leads without ropes and got yourself in trouble … or, you went a hundred feet out once, above a bolt, and a windstorm came along and terrified you.*

Gill: That particular windstorm incident actually occurred. But I don't know if it was quite as horrendous as the stories you've heard. I did a number of first ascents of ridges and faces on the north side of Garnet Canyon – Disappointment Peak, the South Face. At the time I was doing these, this was the major rock-climbing area in the Tetons. I don't know if in recent years very much has been done there or not. Back then, lots of faces and nice sharp ridges had not been climbed. The rock was fundamentally very good in the area, and some of these things went on for a thousand feet. I think I made somewhere between eleven and thirteen first ascents of ridges and faces on the south side of Disappointment Peak. This was in 1957 and in 1958. The climbing in general was not desperate. I did do a lot of leads without very much protection. It was simply the way I was doing things at the time. This was a period when I enjoyed taking a certain amount of risk. The climbs themselves, by and large, were 5.7, 5.8, occasionally 5.9. At this time, 5.9 was the standard of excellence anywhere in the United States, so when we reached that point we felt as though we were doing something. The one climb that you alluded to, going out above the bolt, was the second or third ascent of a ridge called Delicate Arête. This is a sort of uneven arête that at one point about half way up has a broad expanse of face that goes for a hundred and fifty or two hundred feet. There are easy ways of climbing it. You can go to the right of the face and scramble up a gully, or you can climb out on to the face more or less left of centre, or even in the centre of the face, if I remember correctly. There are a number of cracks leading up that provide fairly good protection. And the climbing is probably 5.7 or 5.8. But, if you really want to be a purist, you can go up a kind of blank section that is just to the left of the right hand corner of this face. On the first ascent, I think I used some of Chouinard's very early, prized, knife blade pitons to get protection. The climbing, I guess, at one or two points, gets to be around 5.10 or so. The particular windstorm incident you're alluding to occurred either the second or third time I went up the ridge. There is a bolt that I placed the first time, down at the bottom of the face, to provide an anchor for the belay. I clipped into the bolt with my karabiner, ran my rope through it, and so on. Ritner Walling, I believe, was belaying me at the time. He got himself into a comfortable position, and I took off. It turned out to be a breezy, gusty day, and I got pretty far up this thing, about ninety feet or so above the bolt, and ran into the harder sections of the climb. For some reason, I could not get adequate protection in, so I avoided the 5.10 but still found myself in the middle of a thin, delicate face, perhaps 5.8 – don't ask me how … lunacy, as the wind started to become really bad. At one point I had to plaster myself against the rock. It was a very thin face, there was no protection, and I found myself stuck up there like an insect. As a matter of fact, Ritner later described me as look-ing like an ant trying to avoid being blown off by the wind. I must have stayed there … it seemed like an eternity … couldn't have been more than four or five minutes. But, the wind would be calm, I would start to make a move, and all of a sudden there would be a thirty-or-forty-mile-an-hour gust from the side. Then it would be calm, and there would be a twenty-or-thirty-mile-an-hour gust from the other side. It was really a klutzy climb. It was a very unpleasant experience. I felt as though I was going to come off at any moment. Fortunately I didn't.

Ament: *One account of this incident was that 'Gill got up on a climb, the wind scared him, so he took up bouldering!'*

Gill: That's not too unreasonable a story, actually. Makes a lot of sense at times! That's probably what went through my mind right then. It's not true though. I was bouldering several years before that.

Ament: *Was your hardest route in the Tetons Red Cross Rock, the centre?*

Gill: Yes, provided you are speaking of routes not requiring elimination of certain holds. I've played around on those three little boulders near the ranger station – Falling Ant Slab, Red Cross Rock, and Cut-Finger Rock – for such a long period of time that each boulder has a myriad of routes. It takes a real expert, not just to boulder them, but to decipher which route you're on by eliminating what holds. There may be one or two other little routes in there, where you avoid holds, that are a bit harder than the Red Cross route. But, as for getting up a section of rock without worrying about eliminating holds, well, there just are not very many to eliminate on this one.

Ament: *How did you learn the one-finger, one-arm pull-up?*

Gill: I actually learned it as the result of hearing a rumour. I have no idea whether or not the rumour is true. But, during the year that I spent at the University of Chicago, I went climbing several times with a German mathematician, Helmut Rohrl, a very competent mathematician and quite a good climber. Those were the days, of course, when Hermann-Buhl's reputation was so phenomenal. Helmut had known Buhl – at least in
tangential manner – and told me in one of our conversations that Buhl was able to do a one-finger pull-up. That was the first time I had heard of a climber – or anybody else – doing it. I had been working on one-arm pull-ups. One does those occasionally when training for rope climbing competition. It is an attribute that you develop after a while from climbing the rope. But, as for doing a one-finger, I hadn't really thought much about that. However, I found it to be a very provocative idea. It wasn't that difficult to learn. I think once a person knows how to do a good solid one-arm pull-up, doing it on one finger (and, of course, I ordinarily use the middle finger of my right hand) is not all that hard. I don't do it on a ledge. People have told me that they understand I can do a one-finger pull-up on any finger just on a slim ledge. That is completely false. I was able to do it over a horizontal bar with the middle finger of my right hand, also with the index finger, and I've done it with the middle finger of my left hand. But I never tried pushing it beyond those limits. As to whether I could have gone farther and accomplished more, I don't know. It gets pretty silly after a while, really. The carry-over to climbing is not that great. It's just a little circus gimmick, something to impress other climbers or gymnasts with.

Ament: *One of your most impressive physical accomplishments has been the one-arm front lever. Where did you get the notion to learn that?*

Gill: In Fort Collins in 1968. There were a couple of routes at Horse Tooth Reservoir which required a kind of extended leverage, with your arms out on either side of you, pressing up on your fingertips, the sort of thing that was facilitated by being able to do an iron cross on the rings. I discovered that that type of strength could be cultivated also by doing a regular front lever and then turning and taking one hand off the bar. I'd been doing a front lever for years, but it took a while to learn it with one arm. You turn on your side and start using some of the back muscles that are used when you do the iron cross and other difficult levers. Then again, it was a gimmick. I've always enjoyed doing these gimmicks. They're fun to do and impress people with. I think, however, that the one-arm lever probably contributed to the difficulty I've had with my elbows. For a period of a little over a year, while I was at Fort Collins, I had to give up climbing completely, because I experienced such enormous pain in my elbows, my right elbow in particular. It's an injury that I refer to as climber's elbow. It's a little like tennis elbow, except that it's on the inside of the arm as opposed to the outside. It's an inflammation at the point of attachment of the muscle to the bone, due to severe strain. Or, possibly –one can't tell without surgery – the tendon might actually pull away from the bone a little. In any event, it became so extremely painful that I couldn't do any climbing at all. It reached such a degree that even on an easy climb, if there was a move where I had to pull in, even with my feet on holds, and contract my arm, the pain would become so overwhelming that I would almost black out. And you just can't climb under those circumstances. So I went through a very frustrating period of inactivity. I went to a couple of orthopaedic surgeons and got their advice on it which was, 'We can't do much of anything for this. We can give you a shot of hydrocortisone. But, basically, it'll just have to work its way out.' I laid off for a whole month, to begin with. I didn't do anything with my arm. I practically carried it around in a sling, and that was a big mistake. I didn't use it enough. I thought that the injury had healed at the end of the month, because I could move my arms and could do chin-ups very carefully without it hurting. I went back, and the first climbing trip out, the damned thing pulled and became re-inflamed. It was that terrible pain again. So then I laid off a longer period of time, something like two months, and didn't do much of anything with my arms. When I went back out, I was successful in avoiding pain for a very short period, but then it pulled again on something very easy. At that point I became so disgusted with the whole thing that I simply put away my kletterschuhe, all my climbing equipment, all my chalk, my gymnastics shoes, and gave up any sort of activity that involved the upper torso at all. I did a lot of hiking. I would go out to Horse Tooth Reservoir and run up and down the hillsides to get some exercise and relieve the tension of my school work. I was out of climbing for over a year. I got back into it very gradually. When I started climbing after this long layoff, I was so weak that I could not do five consecutive two-arm pull-ups.

Ament: *Climbers who met you at this time and watched you boulder had a real let-down.*

Gill: My arms were, for me, very atrophied. And I know now that this was a mistake. I should have been taking some sort of therapy and using my muscles more. I should not have let them go like that. It took a while, but I got back into climbing. And I think it was a short time after this that I visited Flagstaff Mountain. There were a number of problems there that I was just not up to at all, certain mantel problems involving a pull against that particular point in my elbow. I guess it was two or three years before I really got back into good shape again. Now I have to take it easy. There's no way that I can go out and boulder every day for a week, because I'm sure this thing would become inflamed again. Not only that, but the rest of my body would probably fall apart. I have to be very careful about warming up. It's getting to the point of absurdity. I'll go out with a young expert climber, and he immediately jumps on the rock, whereas I spend half the time warming up, touching my toes, loosening up, doing push-ups, a few pull-ups. So far, nobody has laughed at me for doing it. It's necessary. I would injure myself if I didn't. I guess ultimately that will be how I end my climbing career. It'll get to the point where I'll spend the entire session warming up! People will take off their kletterschuhe while I'm putting on mine. They'll say, 'Let's go, Gill,' and that'll be it. I'll retire gracefully at that point.

Ament: *You've visited and spent time in a lot of bouldering areas. Would you recall most of these and a few details of some of the routes?*

Gill: I did a lot of bouldering in Georgia, not a lot of exceptionally difficult bouldering, but remember that the standard of excellence in those days was 5.8 or 5.9, and I was certainly doing that on boulders. Some things were probably a little harder. The two years I spent in Alabama, I did some good routes on Shades Mountain outside of Birmingham, routes at a few isolated spots around Tuscaloosa, Alabama, and routes at Desoto Canyon in northern Alabama. This was in 1962 or 1963 ... and 1964. There weren't any B-2's there, I don't believe. Possibly one or two were reasonably difficult B-1. Before that, in 1959, I had climbed some at Devil's Lake, Wisconsin. I was very fortunate at Devil's Lake in that the hard rock climbing that had been done up to that point was around 5.8. I had been doing more difficult things than that in Georgia, so I did more difficult things at Devil's Lake and impressed people in the process, because their standards just hadn't changed much over the years. At Devil's Lake I did, for example, *The Little Flatiron* which is still well regarded. I did the first free ascent of *Congratulation Crack* which I think has become a standard, basic hard climb. I did the *Gill Crack* next to the *Boy Scout Slabs*, near *Brinton's Crack*, also a nose route on the buttress to the right of that which, apparently, is still highly regarded. Many of these routes, incidentally, I did without a top rope, because I was still more or less at that stage where I enjoyed some risk. When I was in the Air Force, stationed in Montana, I drove several times to an area called the Little Rockies and did some bouldering on limestone. There were a few good routes. It was a very obscure, seldom-visited area near Zortman, Montana. At this time, I was doing the bouldering routes in the Tetons and was beginning to do some good routes in the Needles. Then, during the time I was at Murray State University in Kentucky, I spent a lot of time climbing at Dixon Springs and did good routes, one or two of which may be marginal B-2. I made a couple of quick trips to the 'gunks' from New York City in the mid-'60s. There are a number of other widely scattered, obscure areas in which I've bouldered.

Ament: *Is it possible to correspond B-2 with a 5th-class rating?*

Gill: A B-1 might be 5.11, somewhere in there. B-2 is quite a bit harder. And B-3, my feeling is now, should be a completely objective climbing rating. B-3 is something that is done once, is tried frequently, but is not repeated. If it is repeated, then it drops automatically either to B-2 or even B-1. B-1 and B-2 are really the two more or less subjective standards for bouldering, as far as I'm concerned. B-1 is pretty damned hard, and B-2 is really damned hard! And B-3 is an objective standard. I don't think of B-3 as being the supreme technical limit. Once you reach these very esoteric bouldering levels, it becomes increasingly a matter of body size and reach. It is a little absurd to try to keep breaking difficulty down into finer and finer subdivisions. I've had real difficulty with routes that other climbers have done without much effort. So I feel as though, once you get up to those high levels of difficulty, there should be perhaps two, at the most three, grades. Beyond that, there should be a very objective classification which puts climbs in a particular realm of their own without any sort of judgment being required on the part of the climber. You're quite familiar with gymnastics, you know, A-B-C difficulty levels. As far as I know, they haven't enlarged on that. At any rate, getting back to the different areas I have visited, I came to Fort Collins, Colorado, and lived for almost four years, during which time I did a lot of climbing around Horse Tooth Reservoir and some climbing in the granite area on the far hillside. I loved the firm sandstone around the reservoir. And I visited Flagstaff Mountain (Boulder, Colorado) several times but never really concentrated on doing new things at Flagstaff. I've had a lot of fun just doing or attempting to do the things that you pioneered there. The standards, I think, were quite high when I visited Flagstaff (1968–1969). There are several individual areas in Estes Park where I used to enjoy bouldering. Along the Gem Lake Trail – you've been there with me. Over by Window Rock there are some nice boulders. There is one isolated boulder on the way to Bear Lake with several good routes on it. Then, the Hagermeister boulders. I did a number of routes there in the early 1960s. The most pleasant experience I've ever had with bouldering occurred at the Hagermeister boulders. It must have been in the very early 1960s. I drove up for a session of bouldering and got out of the car, took my shoes and chalk and walked over to the standard slab route which is actually a pretty scary little climb, and sat down. When I picked up my shoes to put them on, there was a twenty-dollar bill lying there on the ground. So I put my street shoes back on and put that twenty-dollar bill in my pocket, took my shoes and chalk and went back to the car and drove to town (Estes Park). And that was probably the most enjoyable bouldering session I've ever had. The most rewarding!

Ament: *You mean it was a profitable experience?*

Gill: Indeed! At one time I really enjoyed bouldering on granite, the sort of granite, for example, at Split Rocks. But I'm not all that enthusiastic about it anymore. The very very difficult routes are blank and smooth with a few tiny nubbins. I much prefer to climb on Dakota sandstone. That's my favourite. There are lots of nice holds around and lots of nice acrobatic-gymnastic moves if you're in shape. It's a much more pleasant climbing experience, not so completely frustrating. You walk up to a granite boulder that's egg-shaped, with no visible irregularities or flaws, and know that you are in for a depressing experience. The thing may be only ten feet high, but there may be no way that you can even get off the ground. You can spend a very frustrating half hour or hour just standing there trying to get both feet off the ground simultaneously. At one time, I was glad to go through that experience, because occasionally it would pay off, and I would get up something quite remarkable. Now, I just don't have the patience. I guess I'm just getting too old. I'd much prefer to approach something where I can see a way to get both feet off the ground simultaneously without spending an eternity at it. I've always had a great deal of fun doing overhanging routes on bucket holds. I think many gymnasts would enjoy that sort of activity. It's a real pleasure. There's a big overhang in Dixon Springs State Park in southern Illinois like that. It's got a couple of long, awkward reaches where you almost have to do a one-arm pull-up, so it's a difficult climb. It goes on and on and does have nice big holds. It's a lot of fun. Besides that, if you fall, you take the most delightful swing through the trees!

Ament: *Flagstaff is one place where you can do overhanging faces with buckets.*

Gill: Yes, but I really prefer the Dakota sandstone (Fort Collins, Pueblo) to that on Flagstaff.

Ament: *Dakota sandstone is smoother and doesn't tear your fingers as much.*

Gill: I guess the rock on Flagstaff reminds me of the Needles. I'm not all that crazy about bouldering in the Needles these days. It's very rough on the fingers. You know, if your fingertips have not been conditioned – calloused –on that type of rock, then after the first fifteen or twenty minutes, if you have to try something two or three times and scrape your fingers over it, you're just about shot. You can have all the strength in the world in your shoulders, arms, upper torso, and fingers, but if the pain is so great that you can't put your fingertips on the rock, then you're not going to get very far.

Ament: *I recall when I said, 'Don't worry, John, these pebbles are solid,' and you reached up and grabbed a large pebble that was imbedded seemingly better than any other, and the thing came right out in your hand. I felt stupid.*

Gill: There are always exceptions to the rule.

Ament: *You notice the exceptions more readily when you're a new-comer to an area.*

Gill: I spent years bouldering in the Needles, and the rock is not sandstone, it is a very coarse pegmatite in some ways quite similar to Flagstaff rock, very sharp with little pebbles and crystals sticking out. Frequently you must wrap your hand around a cluster of these things to get a firm handhold. And also, things do come off! I really don't like the sensation of feeling in control of myself on a steep, vertical, or perhaps overhanging face, making a delicate step up, being just fine, reaching for a hold, and all of a sudden finding myself standing on the ground, all because a tiny crystal came off under my foot. These days, I look for very solid rock and stay away from loose stuff. I'm too old to fight it any more. I don't want to fight it.

Ament: *I've found that bouldering can be quite dangerous. In fact, the only times I have been hurt climbing have been while bouldering. But, again returning to the areas in which you have climbed, how much did you do at Veedauwoo, Wyoming?*

Gill: I've been up there, all in all, a dozen times, perhaps more. Rich Borgman and I used to drive up, and I was there with other people at other times. The main problem with Veedauwoo is that the rock formations are more suitable for longer climbs. If you're a rock climber, there are good cracks available. If you're a boulderer, you've got these big, smooth, egg-shaped things. You look at them from ten feet away, and you can't see a single damn hold anywhere. So it's a question of spending half an hour getting both feet off the ground. I've never been greatly in love with the area, but I have done a few decent boulder routes there.

Ament: *The boulders in Yosemite are smooth and rounded. There's a route you could put up there. I've tried it a number of times, because when I see it I imagine you going up it. Also there are a lot of slabs.*

Gill: I'm not crazy about slabs. I prefer something that is vertical or overhanging. I don't think I would enjoy bouldering in Yosemite.

Ament: *Overhanging, swing-type problems and dynamic moves are becoming more and more popular there.*

Gill: To me, that's what bouldering is all about. And that's been my feeling since 1959 or 1960. It is more of a severe athletic activity than classical rock climbing, and you should use more than just your leg muscles, foot muscles, and toes. You *should* use gymnastics, acrobatics, and aerobatics. A good boulder route should require the use of these techniques. I developed the swinging lieback in the early '60s or, actually, before that. This technique can be safely applied to many climbing situations, perhaps not all, but it is certainly well within the domain of bouldering, because it is a nice, acrobatic type of manoeuvre and enables you, frequently, to get over a large section of rock which would be time-consuming and energy-consuming to get over bit by bit in the static fashion.

Ament: *What are your thoughts about lunges where a person shoots with both hands at once, completely out of control, and tries to slap a lichen-covered wall and somehow hang there?*

Gill: Lunging, I think, is a very legitimate bouldering move. Of course, it should be done with some control. It has to be done with some control, otherwise you're going to fall off. For instance, Bob Williams (of Boulder) did a beautiful route like that on the backside of Beer Barrel Rock on Flagstaff.

Ament: *Called Double Clutch.*

Gill: It's a beautiful thing to watch. The state of the art is probably at that point right now – spectacular but controlled lunges. I enjoy doing them on occasion. It's hard to find a route where such a thing is really suitable. But when you find one, you've got something exhilarating. There's an overhang on a little boulder in Cheyenne Canyon near Colorado Springs that you can do that way. There are a number of ways of climbing it statically, but you can also do it dynamically. This provides insight into how bouldering compares with conventional climbing. In rock climbing, the emphasis has always been toward doing something statically. If you can do something dynamically, fine, but, 'you should be able to do it statically.' In bouldering, you might just turn that around. A dynamic move can be a very difficult climbing manoeuvre, depending upon the sort of holds that you are going off of … and landing on. If you're going off a bucket and landing on a bucket, it might not be all that hard. The Fatted Calf boulder west of Pueblo has a dynamic route throwing you completely off the rock at one point for a split second. And you do not launch yourself from huge holds. You must fling yourself off in such a manner that you can get your hand over the top of the rock rather than just shoot out into space. You go off of small holds, a lieback on a sort of flange. And your feet are not on horizontal holds at all. They're on sloping friction holds. It requires a lot of timing and practice. It can be a very pretty thing to watch and a very stimulating thing to do.

Ament: *Would you mention a few of your climbing companions and a few impressions you have had of each?*

Gill: I guess I've been very fortunate. The people that have bouldered with any degree of seriousness, whom I have been acquainted with, have all developed beautifully. And I've always managed to pick something up from them, some little bit of technique, some form, style, things that are difficult to put your finger on. It's always been an educational experience for me when I go out with a young climber who's quite good. I met Rich Goldstone when I was at the University of Chicago in 1959 and met with him off and on during the summers until about 1964 or 1965. He progressed tremendously during that time. He was a reasonably good climber when I first met him. He was young and immature but, apart from that, a good climber. He progressed into an absolutely beautiful boulderer and rock climber, particularly good at balance work. I think I picked up some pointers on good form by just watching Rich climb. I think he learned something from me too, but I always learn something from the people I'm with. When I meet a young climber who wants to learn how to do hard bouldering, I never view it as strictly a one-sided educational enterprise. I try to provide an adequate example so that the person – if he has the basic talent – will be able to emulate what I do and be able to avoid mistakes that I make. By observing me, a lot of these people progress rapidly. As they progress they develop unique styles, and by absorbing these I am able to correct my own deficiencies. It's an on-going process. But I wouldn't say that I take a climber and mould him. These people, practically all of them, have an excellent reservoir of raw talent. They watch me, and perhaps I give them some impetus, but they develop on their own. Rich Borgman, with whom I climbed at Fort Collins for several years, was an absolutely superlative climber. I can't think of any individual aspect of his climbing which impressed me more than his overall ability. I'm sure I picked up something by osmosis by just being with him and watching. I couldn't put my finger on it now if I had to. But, after I had climbed with Rich for a while I was a better climber. I had been able to observe someone rather than develop by myself, in a vacuum. He's got a lot of drive. You yourself have very beautiful form. I have always been impressed by the smoothness with which you climb and the difficult boulder problems you have established. I'm sure that observing you has affected my climbing substantially. Bob Williams, of Boulder, wasn't doing that much bouldering when I first met him, but he instantly became exceptional at it. I learned quite a bit by going out with Bob. In his case, I think I can put my finger on something that I learned. Some climbers have a very static technique, others have a very dynamic technique. Mine tends to be more dynamic than static. Most rock climbers have a static technique. However, Bob Williams struck a beautiful balance between the two, the best I think I have ever seen. He could combine static and dynamic moves and get up such difficult things doing it. That's not to say that he was not excellent when it came to a purely dynamic manoeuvre, as *Double Clutch* indicates. When Bob and I bouldered together, I would approach a problem one way, and he would approach it another. Quite frequently, his technique would turn out to be the best. It was always some sort of amazing combination – depending upon the complexity of the problem – of dynamic and static climbing. For example, he polished off the bottom section of the north overhang of *The Scab* in this manner. It is a very difficult route in the Needles. That must have been eight years ago. He did it by pulling himself into a chin-up position, holding himself there momentarily, and then more or less bouncing up to another hold. This was one of his strong points, to be able to hang on very tiny holds in very good control, make a sort of bounce, reach very far up from the initial set of holds to something else which might not be terribly big itself, hang on there, and if necessary repeat the procedure. I had done the bottom part of *The Scab* an entirely different way, using a purely dynamic technique. So, those are four individuals who are, in my mind, quite outstanding climbers from whom I learned a great deal.

Ament: *You have undoubtedly had some novel or bizarre experiences. Care to relate any that you might remember?*

Gill: I remember when I thought that Bob Williams – not the one I've just been talking about, but my friend from Northwestern University, who is an older gentleman but quite a competent climber – was going to be wiped out on the Needle in Estes Park. It's not a very fond memory, but one which lingers, believe me. I had just finished working out the first no-hands ascent of the Needle, which was a little hairy. We had both gotten to the top and were coming down. About a third of the way down, Bob's piton hammer, which was sticking out of his back pocket, got caught on the rock and tossed him around. He went spinning off toward the edge of an overhang on the backside of the spire. Just before he went over the edge, he reached up and grabbed a ledge. He would only have fallen about twenty feet, but I suspect that he would have been killed. It was not a nice, soft, sandy landing. There were jagged boulders and trees. He was very sedate about the whole thing. It didn't seem to bother him particularly. It upset me so much that I didn't want to do any more bouldering the rest of the day. I recall being somewhat surprised the day up in Fort Collins when you landed on your tailbone, because I was sure that you were going to make it, and of course you subsequently did make it with a great deal of ease. But something happened, something that will happen to any climber, no matter how good he is, now and then. His foot will slip, or his hand. Something just doesn't work quite right. But, I was surprised and dismayed. Even though I was standing pretty close, I didn't have a chance to spot you. I was quite happy that you hadn't damaged yourself seriously. I've had days like that, plenty of them. I don't like to talk about them, but there are days when I can't even tie my shoes correctly, much less do a climb. I recall an interview that you gave, and you made a point about being in and out of shape with the regularity of a yo-yo. I can sympathise, because I've had exactly that experience. It's one thing that has always annoyed me about my climbing. I like to refer to it as 'artistic inconsistency'. An artistic person can have his flares and do extremely well sometimes but not at others. However, this may be merely a euphemism for a baser capriciousness. I'm never quite sure what kind of day I'm going to have. Sometimes when I hit it, as the expression goes, I do extremely well. On other occasions, I've been known to do very poorly on just mediocre rock.

Ament: *The worst times are usually what climbers remember. Unfortunately, people whom you boulder with are bound to want to make a judgment about you.*

Gill: I prefer to climb with someone who is a friend, such as you and the people I have mentioned, because I am more relaxed. Perhaps there isn't such a fierce, competitive urge. I like a bouldering session where you can afford to laugh at yourself and laugh at each other. I'll have to admit that, in some instances in the past eight or ten years, I have felt a bit like a classical, old, western gunfighter who is always being goaded into a shoot-out on Main Street at some bouldering sessions.

Ament: *You want to have the right to be able to 'fail' if you're so inclined.*

Gill: Especially because I know that sometimes I am going to fail.

Ament: You don't want to have to worry about someone saying, 'He didn't do it first try.'

Gill: Right. It's the climber's cardinal sin: vanity. A lot of us are cursed with it. However, it is instructive to recall another definition of the word – futility. I'd rather go out with a friend, an acquaintance with whom I can relax a little, as opposed to someone to whom I must prove my absurdly impractical abilities all over again.

Ament: *You apparently do not have a desire to travel to every top bouldering area and try each of their hardest routes.*

Gill: I've never felt a desire to do that. I've always had the ability to stand apart from bouldering and, particularly, climbing. I've never actually considered myself a genuine, bona fide rock climber, even though I've done quite a bit of it. I'm quite thankful to be able to stand apart and look not only at other climbers but at myself, my moods, my interests …

Ament: *The depth of climbing lies in its personal, individualistic aspects. Popular values, dictated by the masses, discourage creativity. Unique individuals are given definitions, and to be defined, I think, is to be degraded.*

Gill: I agree with that. Climbing is a very personal experience. Much of the joy of the art arises from the spontaneity which infuses it. It is precisely this characteristic that frustrates pigeonholing.

Ament: *One day at Fort Collins, you and I climbed easy things and ran around on some cliffs just playing follow-the-leader, unrestricted by convention.*

Gill: My climbing philosophy has more or less stabilized at this point in life. I enjoy very competitive bouldering on occasion, not always. I get quite a bit of satisfaction out of reclimbing routes that I have established. I've never felt totally compelled to do something that somebody else has done. I've just never felt this compulsion, never felt the necessity, to be accepted in a certain way by doing a certain thing. I think I've been fairly independent. Well, I've had to be to be a boulderer. In the 1950s, you had to be pretty darn independent to specialise in bouldering, and you had to suffer the mild derision of conventional climbers.

Ament: *Are there goals which you have not achieved in bouldering, for example, routes which you wish you had made or hope to do yet, someday?*

Gill: None at all. From time to time I've been locked in the grips of a consuming passion for this route or that. But these have been periods of short duration. I don't hold a grudge against a nemesis. I've always enjoyed hiking. That's been an entirely separate activity for me within the mountain realm. When I go hiking I usually don't even think about bouldering. I can walk beneath a beautiful boulder, and it will catch my eye just for a moment. I'd rather look at the flowers, the trees, the birds, and stop to get a drink of water out of a stream. That type of physical and aesthetic activity I appreciate as much as acrobatic exercise. I also like to do long, relatively easy solo climbs. There are several places around Pueblo where I can climb several hundred feet up large pillars and buttresses. There is a tremendous amount of exposure, but the holds are all there, and fairly large. I like the sense of solitude, but without an accompanying sense of desperation. I like to be able to stop practically anywhere I am climbing and look around, look out over the valley, listen to a bird, look at a bush or a tree …

Ament: *What advice would you give to climbers as to how to progress?*

Gill: It depends upon basic bodily structure and physiology as to how one can progress. You have to keep in mind what your end goals are. With regard to bouldering, the person is going to have to develop strength. I firmly believe that most people who wish to pursue bouldering can really benefit from formal gymnastics: rope climbing, still rings, parallel bars, some high bar, free exercise … I think that these are excellent activities with regard to developing acrobatic dexterity, poise, gracefulness, and balance, various attributes which a good boulderer should possess. I personally have never used weights for training except to do a one-arm pull-up with twenty to thirty pounds of weight in the other hand. I've avoided doing well-regimented exercises, the classical curls and military presses. I'm not going to emphatically say that a person would not progress quite nicely using these means. But it depends upon the individual very much.

What's worked best for me has been a combination of actual bouldering and certain forms of gymnastics. The weakest link between the climber and the rock is the fingers. Most climbing does require finger strength. However, you know from your own experience that there are a lot of crack climbs that do not directly involve finger strength but rather certain cross-pressure strengths utilising various upper torso muscles. Unfortunately, finger strength is probably the most difficult to develop and keep. It is the first thing to go with increased age. I'm thirty-nine now, and my finger strength has not diminished severely over the last ten or fifteen years, but I can't be too optimistic about the future. There are exercises that I have used to develop my fingers – fingertip chins on doorjambs and, ultimately, one-arm chins on the first joint of the fingers. This, I want to point out, tends to develop power more than stamina. In most instances, a boulderer is concerned with a sudden burst of power, as opposed to long-term stamina, but not always. The sort of strength one develops when working on the still rings seems to carry over to climbing. It gives you a certain amount of poise when under stress, on overhangs for example. For a number of years, the sort of gymnastics that I did was geared to routines done in actual competition on the various pieces of apparatus. I was able to do butterfly mounts on the rings moderately easily and an iron cross. I did an inverted cross on occasion. Over the past few years, I've gotten away from gymnastics and at present don't do any. I haven't climbed the rope in about ten years. I do traverses across long doorjambs when they are available. I'm getting a little out of shape on front levers, haven't done one recently. I used to do quite a bit of hand balancing but don't do any now. I haven't done a handstand in perhaps three years. Upon occasion I will do – or at least attempt to do – a one-arm mantel shelf on a low rock wall. Just one or two of these per session, I have found, keeps me in fairly good shape as far as that sort of pressing is concerned. I've never been terribly good at mantels, one of the reasons being that my legs are too long.

Ament: *We have commented that bouldering is an art, that it is born of discipline and feeling. How far can we go with the concept of bouldering as art?*

Gill: I would not want to add too much of a sophisticated veneer to it. At one time, I quite seriously did consider it an art form similar to ballet or formal, competitive gymnastics. When one sees good bouldering, one sees a graceful display of athletic ability. There is the same sort of precision that is apparent in good dance, the same sort of balance, coordination, and strength. I've found bouldering to be therapeutic. It might be interpreted as a kinaesthetic art form. An observer can, even with very little knowledge of climbing, appreciate the artistry in bouldering, just as a person unacquainted with gymnastics is able to appreciate artistic composition and grace in a good exhibition.

Ament: *Do you feel a need to express yourself in bouldering? Is there something living in us that you might say, 'asks' to be put on to the canvas?*

Gill: That's a very interesting analogy between bouldering and painting. I suppose one does, by pioneering a route, establish something upon a natural backdrop, something that is not visible but was not there before except in a very hypothetical sense. That interpretation has a certain amount of validity. Yet, I tend to think of bouldering more in terms of the pure physical activity involved, the joy of movement, the joy of doing something well. In addition, I think of it as the physical counterpart of doing a chess problem. A good bouldering route is not one where the sequence of holds is perfectly obvious. It should be difficult to discover the correct sequence, and it should be difficult to execute that sequence. I would also compare it to mathematics. I'm a mathematician. I do mathematical research, and you might be surprised by the very close parallel that exists between the two pursuits – one, apparently purely intellectual, the other apparently purely physical. In both instances, a person stands more or less at a frontier. This ties in with the remark I made previously about not feeling compelled to do problems which other people have established. I think of bouldering as a physical counterpart of creative mathematics. It is enlightening to follow the proof of an established theorem, but far more satisfying to discover a new theorem. It is a creative enterprise, and I do not believe in painting a picture by numbers. One takes a blank canvas and does something original. That really sums up quite a bit of my attitude toward bouldering.

In both bouldering and mathematics, you stand upon the threshold of something new, something that requires not only brute force (whether it be physical or intellectual force) but a certain insight, a certain quantum jump from point to point. When a good mathematician establishes or formulates mathematics, he makes a quantum jump from the frontier of knowledge in one area of mathematics to a new frontier. His intuition bridges the gap, he rarely goes step by step – at least initially. The same is true in bouldering. I don't mean making a physical jump, although sometimes that helps! But, when I approach a boulder that has not been climbed and is apparently devoid of holds, I view it as the same sort of challenge as an untested area of mathematics. There is something there that can be created, possibly, if one uses insight, intuition, etc., in order to make this quantum jump. One discovers that the bouldering route can be accomplished not by looking at each minute hold, foot by foot, but by looking at the overall route. One gets an instinctive feeling that it can be done and then starts looking closely for and at holds. Once you've made this intuitive jump, you test it. You try to back it up with logic. You connect the point at which you want to arrive to the closest point on the frontier of knowledge by a chain of logic. You have an instinctive feeling that the thing will go, that you can establish this painting, if you like, on this natural backdrop. Once you have convinced yourself intuitively that this is the case, you start looking for the holds, and you usually find that they are there. Of course, I think that feeling optimistic, if your instinct tells you there's something there, gives you a psycho-physical boost that will perhaps get you past a thin spot or two which you might not have considered possible looking at it piece by piece.

Ament: *In bouldering, are these quantum jumps, as you call them, more difficult to substantiate? Is there more romance?*

Gill: In mathematics, the language is extremely formal, and you face the restrictions of the language – in going from one point to another. The chain of logic may be, intellectually, extremely difficult to establish. The intellectual aspect of bouldering is a bit like trifling compared with mathematics, and, physically, mathematics is insignificant compared with bouldering. I don't really think of bouldering as being terribly romantic, although it is imaginative. Rock climbing was romantic at one time, during a certain golden period, perhaps during the 1950s when it was developing through the 5.7, 5.8, 5.9 stages and a relatively small number of people were involved. Climbers did not concentrate heavily on equipment then, and when one went out to do a climb there was no certainty that he was going to make it. Nowadays if you take enough equipment, and there's always enough equipment available, you're going to get up anything unless you apply certain artificial restrictions. Even with such restrictions the romance has faded, because of the popularity of the sport.

Perhaps this is just an aging boulderer's nostalgia, but I do, in a way, look back upon that period of time when I was getting started climbing as a romantic age. Maybe it was just my immaturity at the time. But, I think it wasn't all that. I can still pull out the old American Alpine Journals and read, for example, about the first ascent of the North Face of the Grand Teton and about – who was it – Pownall stuffing his gloves in the crack. There was a sense of adventure, a certain flair. There was not a reliance upon bolts, and there was not hexagonal nut No. 1, No. 2, No. 3. It was a good adventure among companions, more akin to something out of a classical adventure novel than anything you see these days. Of course, the levels of difficulty are astronomical now compared with the early '50s, but I think there was a much more romantic feeling then. You felt that you were explorers of a sort, charting new realms. The climbing environment has changed so drastically that it is difficult to compare the climbing of the early '50s with that of the early or middle '70s. The accomplishments of the early '50s were more unique. And perhaps it's because of this uniqueness and the fact that the general public, even the more athletic outdoor types, were not as aware of mountaineering, that it was more of an adventure. Physically, the frontiers were not as difficult to advance then as they are now. But, I think that this allowed for the more adventurous, romantic spirit and the idea of just going out and having a good time.

Nowadays, when you are on the frontier of knowledge, or you're on the frontier of some area of climbing, it's a pretty serious enterprise to make any advancement. The same is true in mathematics. In the days when mathematics was just being formulated, it would not seem it was any big deal to go from one logical step to another. It was probably more of an ordeal than we would suspect, however, from our vantage point in time. But, at present the frontiers in the areas of specialisation are so extreme that it does require quite a large intellectual commitment, time, and energy to make any advancement.

Ament: *Climbing sometimes seems to be taking a step backwards in that climbers are desperate to make their name in a world where it is harder and harder to be original.*

Gill: I think anyone who is engaged in climbing has always had at least a side interest in making a name for himself. There's no doubt about that. Even with all this sense of fun and adventure I mentioned, there was that element to it. You'd be doing something new and somewhere in the course of history it would be acknowledged. I believe that anybody who pushes a frontier, no matter whether it be athletic or intellectual, wants to receive recognition for doing that particular thing. In the old days, everyone knew everyone else who was climbing. Now that's far from true.

Ament: *Henry Barber once suggested to me that if bouldering was considered the purest form of climbing, you would be at the highest peak.*

Gill: That's very flattering, and I feel much honoured that Henry would make such a statement. I do think that bouldering is a very pure form of climbing; however, there are certain psychological obstacles that one must overcome when doing longer climbs. There are a host of things that bouldering does not touch upon at all. It is motion. It is the accomplishment of something physically very difficult. It is a distillation of the acrobatic part of climbing and, hence, only a part of the actual rock-climbing experience. I do not have any commitment to rock climbing. I am, quite literally, rusty at putting in protection, especially nuts and the more contemporary forms of protection. I definitely feel that it is doing a disservice to a great number of really excellent climbers to make that very flattering comment about me. I do feel as though I am perhaps the most prominent boulderer in this country, and I think I am a competent one. As to whether or not I am the best in the country, let alone the world, that is a point to be argued. There are a number of rock acrobats who are beautiful climbers with excellent abilities. A few of these individuals do things that are far beyond the realm of bouldering, too. Free soloing, for example, is an outgrowth of bouldering. I haven't had very much experience free soloing things of the level of difficulty that are free soloed these days. There is one exception to that, and that's the Thimble. It's really an exception in my whole climbing career. I did solo, in the early 1960s, several 5.10 routes, but I did them with a rope and protection. Bouldering is both a part and an abstraction of rock climbing.

Ament: *It has been pointed out by Royal that, paradoxically, a number of climbers who have done the three-thousand-foot wall of El Capitan cannot do many of your ten-foot boulder problems.*

Gill: It is paradoxical only if one feels that a person at that end of the spectrum should be equally competent at the opposite end of the spectrum.

Ament: *John Gill and Sir Edmund Hillary ...*

Gill: We both enjoy hiking. I suspect that if we were to meet on common ground, it would be because I have activities in the outdoor world other than bouldering. He would probably be slightly amused by my boulder problems, for no other reason than that they are completely dwarfed by the sort of enterprises that he has experience with. It might be difficult to get a conversation started, other than on some mutual ground such as hiking, because too often in the past – I don't know if this is true anymore – being a mountaineer implied getting to a summit … in capital letters. The means by which one got to the summit – as long as it involved climbing (in the technical sense of the word) and you didn't take a helicopter to the top – were somewhat immaterial. In bouldering, you're as much, if not more, concerned with form, style, elegance, and route difficulty as you are with getting to the top. Good heavens, there are all sorts of routes that don't even end up on the tops of boulders. Traverses, for example, and routes on cliffs. There are exceptional climbs that go part way up a cliff. You run into a blank wall, jump off, and that's the end of the bouldering problem. I've spoken before with mountaineers about this sort of thing. It's usually difficult for them to adjust to a feeling for the small when they've been so concerned with the large. One little epigram which Chouinard once applied to bouldering was, 'Instant suffering.' And I'll agree. It's as if you take a lengthy climb and sort of squeeze it down into one or two moves. To compensate for decreased length you increase the difficulty. Many rock climbers look down their noses, so to speak, at bouldering. To a great many rock climbers it is precisely what it has been traditionally, and that is, a form of training. They see it as nothing more. Well, of course it is a lot more. It does have validity in its own right also. It has its compensations, its devotees. It doesn't depend upon rock climbing for its existence in any way, shape, or form. Rock climbing could completely vanish and bouldering would still exist. Perhaps we're talking about the same medium but different perspectives.

Ament: *What are your thoughts on the use of aids, such as shoe rosin, in climbing?*

Gill: One argumentative topic – not necessarily everywhere – but you see it in climbing magazines, etc. – is the use of chalk. I feel a little bit responsible for this, because I probably was the first to use chalk for climbing. I got it from gymnastics in the late 1950s. I've used it a little bit on longer climbs. I can understand some of the feelings that a more traditional rock climber might have against the use of chalk. He wants to go out and have a romantic adventure, like the guys in the old days. Yet, he has a guidebook to tell him the grade and what size nut to take along. But, I can sympathise with him. I still use chalk and probably always will, because I don't think it's improper to use on boulders. Now you mentioned that some climbers are using rosin on their shoes? This actually, in a sense, destroys the route, and is not a proper piece of technical paraphernalia to use in any area of climbing. Chalk can be washed away very easily, can be scraped off with a soft wire brush, looks a little ugly at times, but just is not all that big a deal.

I'm afraid the controversy which has arisen around the use of chalk is symptomatic of perhaps the particular state that climbing is in right now. It's in a rather troubled state. One of the reasons for this is that young, aggressive climbers are not finding it easy to make a reputation for themselves. They are resorting to more and more artificial means – desperate tactics, even lies – in order to establish their name. Well, I don't think that the use of lies in mountaineering is anything new. I certainly encountered them when I began climbing. But, the desperation has reached a rather high level in the last couple of years. It's because there is a glut of climbers, and they are, basically, very good. What one of them can do, a host of others can do. And how can you be an individual under such circumstances? One way to be an individual, to stand out, is to start an argument or to engage in an argument and take a position. This adds a sort of literary quality to your philosophical bulk, to your climbing image. I've given up reading at least one of the very prominent mountaineering magazines, because it's simply full of what appear to me to be very childish arguments.

Ament: *How do you feel about the put-down, 'Only a boulderer'?*

Gill: I think that most of the people who make remarks such as that, for one reason or another, simply don't want to spend the time and effort that it takes to be a good boulderer and to rise to the levels of expectation in bouldering. Only a boulderer? That title doesn't bother me at all. I readily admit that I am. It's a sport I enjoy. As a matter of fact, I'm a little uncomfortable with the fact that there are so many people now that do take bouldering seriously. The only way to feel a sense of romance, I guess, is when you're one of a small minority. There is heavily increasing competition, and I suspect that it enters into my feelings. At least at the present time a person can stand out as an individual in the bouldering world. I don't know whether that will be true in five years. It's not so easy to demonstrate the distinction between your style and someone else's when you're doing a longer route, so you have to resort to, 'Well, he used a nut here where I didn't use one.'

Ament: *There are large numbers of good climbers today, but climbers of the '50s and '60s were so stylistic, so set apart. When you see Chuck Pratt climb, his approach is distinct, unlike anyone else's. The first thing you notice about Tom Higgins is his footwork. There is something eye-catching there. Royal is a remarkable individual, always will be, in my estimation. If Kor and Dalke were to get back to climbing, I think they would stand out. How many climbers could be so brilliant and remain as low profile as Tom Frost or Dave Rearick? Fewer of the top climbers today have qualities that are that peculiar.*

Gill: Yet, they're awfully good. Perhaps that's their problem. In the past, there were a few that were very good, and these people would stand out at that time, and perhaps they still stand out, even if they no longer climb at those levels. They have been established in the archives of rock climbing history.

Ament: *It is a natural inclination to question the merit of more recent climbing achievements. Climbers today are a kind of offspring of a collective effort. They have been able to use the mass amount of information and grow with the help of mass mentality. A case in point might be that there will be twenty people in a small climbing community, and none of them will be able to touch a 5.10 move, let's say, because it's too hard for them, they've tried it, they can't do it. But if one of them reaches within himself and searches and goes beyond his mental blocks and his own kind of superficial awareness and rises above – kind of spiritually – and discovers that he can climb 5.10, even 5.11, and then progresses radically, well, magically, and I've seen this time and again, all the other climbers can suddenly do 5.10 and 5.11. They'll follow right in his footsteps.*

Gill: I recognise that too.

Ament: *The individual possibly unlocks a sort of door that they are not able to unlock themselves, and it's what separates him as the artist, whereas they are the followers with that mass mentality to, in a sense, regulate them. There are a lot of new and talented climbers, yet Higgins is one who has shown them something. He has brought a kind of knowledge into being. It makes us wonder how many good climbers today could have done as well ten years ago with the same physical make-up.*

Gill: That's all absolutely true, but there will be pioneers of each new age, also. Henry Barber is a notable example. It's somehow knowing that you're going to be able to progress, in a larger arena of competition, beyond those limits which the group has, in effect, established.

Ament: *Something may be created, then it is natural and relatively easy for it to be copied. But, people may lose sight of the original and not know or care that they were ever inspired by it. Climbers today appear to have duplicated or surpassed the achievements of climbers ten years or twenty years ago, yet in our minds we ask, 'Have they?'*

Gill: Most top-notch climbers ten years ago actually crossed the frontier and contributed something to climbing. There are a lot of really bright, talented people whom we expect to see doing that now. Those of us who are older say to ourselves, 'My gosh, if these people had been around when I was starting climbing they would have completely eclipsed me.' But, maybe it isn't true. Maybe they would have only achieved to the level of expectation at that time. And it would have taken something else for them to go beyond. This is true also in mathematics. Quite frequently, in an area of investigation, a number of top-notch researchers will be stymied. But then somebody will come along and make that quantum jump, and they'll say, 'Look at this, we've never seen this before. Looks weird.' Then they'll start making the connection and say, 'Oh, well, it's really quite easy.' And all of a sudden everybody is at that advanced point. I've gone out with an exceptionally good boulderer who has always been able to duplicate practically anything. Yet when we would look at something brand new together that had not been done and I would expect him to perform, he wouldn't, for some reason. But, once the route was done he'd do it beautifully. There is that distinction. You look at the climbing population and see what talent there is, yet climbers are not making these big steps. A lot of that raw talent is technical expertise but perhaps lacks the spark, that vital force …

Ament: *Magic …*

Gill: Schazammmm, huh? To carry it beyond the frontiers. Maybe it isn't that climbing is going backwards. It's just that, with our experience, we think that standards should be going forward faster.

Ament: *We want to give new climbers credit when they do things, and we enjoy most of them as people, yet on another level we resent them when they invariably set themselves above climbers who came before them, because certain strides have been made.*

Gill: That's right. When they started climbing they were taken into an area and told, 'Now here is a 5.10. You're a talented person. Watch me climb it.' That individual climbs it and says, 'Now you do it.' And the person does it and says, 'If I had been around fifteen years ago, just think of the marvellous things I would have done!' As a matter of fact, that individual may have lacked the essential spark to go beyond the established norm. It seems absolutely trite that somebody would push 5.12. Perhaps there is an embarrassingly strong norm in the rock-climbing community which provides a measure of restriction and keeps some individuals from progressing.

Ament: *People such as Robbins and Pratt, who have moved through the generations and are now a part of the new one, who remain actively involved, retain their unique characteristics partly by setting their own rules. For example, Robbins has climbed a lot in tennis shoes. He has done the Direct North Buttress of Middle Cathedral Rock in Yosemite and lots of other 5.10 cracks in his little white Tretorns. Pratt remains completely enigmatic, avoiding the public eye and climbing circles. He doesn't care to let the world know what he's up to. He seldom talks about his achievements, seldom visits Camp 4, and doesn't bother himself with competitive, self-perpetuating games.*

Gill: One point may be that they have such stature that they can get away with changing the rules. A young, immature climber trying to do the same, well, people would laugh at him, probably. But, when Royal Robbins starts wearing tennis shoes, people say, 'How interesting.' That's the way I started climbing – with basketball shoes – but I sure didn't get rave notices! It's true, these people were the innovators at the time, and they haven't lost their innovative spark. You yourself are developing an interesting and innovative talent in writing, a talent which can be widely appreciated, much more so than technical advancement. It is your own craft. You have that spark of true individualism and initiative that enables you to set the rules of the game, so to speak, and abide by them and feel comfortable doing so. It is more and more difficult to do truly individual things, to take initiative and find areas in which climbing can move – new philosophical directions. What you have to do is grow older. You have to have had the spark initially and had enough intestinal fortitude to exhibit it. Then you have to grow older.

Ament: *What do you feel about the inevitable jealous comments climbers make about other climbers?*

Gill: We have got to be tolerant. There are going to be injustices perpetrated, and we're just going to have to accept them. I no longer have any scruples about the things I climb, so there are the inevitable criticisms. I've been annoyed by climbers who have said, 'Oh, you did that? How many tries did it take?' Even if I'm going up something lengthy with a top rope, I can get all the way up to within three feet of the top, and if I feel as though I haven't done it smoothly, I'm just as likely to back off and swing down the darn thing as I am to continue climbing. But, of course, other parties that are watching feel as though you are on trial. You just have to be psychologically strong enough to understand their perspective and not let it bother you. Most of the misunderstandings in climbing and bouldering stem from the fact that the different participants have different feelings about the ethics of the situation, and these feelings are not communicated.

Ament: *Some climbers are unable to draw a distinction between reality and myth. When they see you boulder, they are disappointed if you do not perform as they would have you perform in their imagination. You don't match the show of the mythical figure. Mythology itself has become a topic of interest in assorted climbing journals and books. Part of the climbing world seems to be attempting to break through the myths and foster other ones. Some mythology is meaningful, I believe. Apparently you learned a one-finger pull-up because of a myth.*

Gill: It's these myths that spur climbers on. It's valuable mythology, necessary for the advancement of the art. Myths are a binding and procreative force. With regard to myth destruction, perhaps the sheer pressure of numbers now forces climbers to take out their competitive spirit on their predecessors, because these are the people who are the least able or willing to defend themselves. Essentially, younger individuals have to overcome the myth. They accomplish as much as the mythical figure did, then attempt to go beyond. That supposedly diminishes the effect of the mythical figure, and it tends to promote that individual's image.

Ament: *It would have been interesting to know Oliver Perry-Smith or have some real insight into the level at which he climbed in 1906.*
Gill: He was a true pioneer.
Ament: *T.M. Herbert has an outstanding ability to make people laugh. You're around him a little while and begin to appreciate climbing all over again. He is definitely one of these …*
Gill: … personalities which are not sterile. What you're looking for, really, is creativity.

Ament: *Some people express their creativity by hammering holds off of routes they can't do. If they can't do them, then they don't want anyone else to do them either. Or they hammer holds into routes to make them possible.*

Gill: That's just a minor degrading aspect of the sport. With as many people involved in it as there are, you've got to expect this kind of development too. The fact that we are getting this diversity should make it apparent that climbing is more than just establishing a better decimal system. I think now that we are seeing – at least with some climbers – the possibility of a turning inward and maybe a spiritual awareness by turning inward. Perhaps climbing can be something not so devastatingly technical in the future.

Ament: *Tom Higgins seems to have mastered having fun at climbing while keeping climbing in a good perspective with the rest of his life. He is ahead of climbing, above it, and seeing through it.*

Gill: That's certainly a gift. He's a beautiful climber, beautiful to watch. You know, I think that it is really the climber who determines whether or not climbing or bouldering is to be considered an art form or something purely athletic. With Higgins, I would think it would lean far in the direction of being an art form, because when you watch him climb everything is so smooth, and the movements are well formed. There are other climbers who give you entirely the opposite feeling, that it is a purely technical event. I would suspect that this would be true of the Russian attitude toward climbing, the speed, go from point A to point B in X number of seconds and try to beat that.

Ament: *Or the bouldering competitions. You raise a hand to signal that you're at the top, the stopwatch clicks off, and you fall!*

Gill: It's best, though, that climbing does allow these varied interpretations. It has discipline and also a tremendous degree of freedom. Philosophically speaking, I like your phrase about getting more out of less. You wouldn't want to mandate this to be the goal of all climbers. But, for a certain segment of climbers, it is a very admirable goal. It leads to an inward appraisal, taking stock of oneself and one's philosophy about climbing. Another interesting aspect of climbing that I've always found very appealing is that it does tend to merge body and mind. So many things we do isolate body and mind. For example, in mathematics or physics, you're almost sure to isolate your body from your mind.

Ament: *Chess ...*

Gill: On the other hand, if you go into a gymnasium and get on a tread wheel or something like that, well, that also, as far as I am concerned, is isolation. But climbing draws it together.

Ament: *It can draw you together with your companions too.*

Gill: It sure can. It acts as a sort of catalyst to homogenize the various facets of a human being. One knowledgeably practices climbing and attacks a pitch with his sense of reason, pulling his body along after him for X number of seasons. In time, he is eventually able to put out of his mind what he has been instructing himself to do, because at that point instinct begins to take over. After a period of time, you can walk up to a rock – it's like your approach to chess – and you see the problem without having to closely inspect the individual parts. Applying your intellect to problems, thinking about them, is actually an intermediate step in the development of technique in climbing. You want to reach a point where it fits together in your subconscious, and then you climb it instinctively. I've heard several prominent climbers remark that in order to really climb effectively and naturally one must erase society's conditioning and try to remember what we knew instinctively as children. I don't buy that. Children simply don't climb that well. Sophisticated rock technique is not a part of our primal heritage. On the other hand, growing up in society, the pure, childlike play experience, is drummed out of a person. By some hook or crook, you have to go back and recapture that in order to get the most out of climbing and to find it intrinsically rewarding. Now this is easy to solve if you just remain immature all your life!

Ament: *I occasionally have a dream that someone I know is supernatural. It's kind of crazy, but I had one such dream about you the other night. I was watching you climb, seeing you in profile. It was as if the wall fell away far below. You were high up, but I was to one side and could safely watch. You were climbing and fell off, because it was too hard. Anyone else would have been killed, but you disappeared downward and landed on a tiny ledge a few inches wide that no one else would have been able to stop on. I poked my head around the corner of the wall and saw you standing down there. You had seen the ledge, calculated the distance to it, and while you were climbing had decided that it was, in essence, the same as the ground. You knew confidently that you would be able to land on it should you fall. You dropped about twenty feet on to it, catching it with one leg and standing there. I was saying, 'Wow, he is supernatural!'*

Gill: I would have been saying 'Wow', too!

Ament: *I suppose this dream is reflective of a feeling I have about certain climbers. I refer to their sort of light, weightless quality which allows them to outdo themselves. Sammy Reshevsky, at eight years of age, was a grandmaster chess player. You can barely talk at that age, but for some reason the little runt had the gift of chess. He was touring the country, giving simultaneous exhibitions. His nose would come up to the height of the tables, while experienced players would peer down at him in amazement as he checkmated them. It's something to think about. Perhaps climbers are at times able to summon up some sort of inner power. Maybe it is psychic phenomena. Or, possibly their energy level is disturbed by some inner or outer influence, but the climber has something that he expresses, consciously or unconsciously, which helps him climb.*

The untrained eye is delighted or bemused while observing such a climber. However, only with a few climbers have I been able to detect anything like this that is substantial.

Gill: Climbing is an extremely complex activity. In climbing, some people may have an added knack for integrating every facet of the experience. With all the apparent developments and advances in the Soviet Union and elsewhere, the moving of objects, telekinesis, you wonder if some climbers don't unknowingly have psychic skills. It would be interesting if one could devise a test and determine whether or not they do. Perhaps a simple test would work, where you have them stand on a scale. Depending upon some undetermined set of factors – environment, mood, etc., their weight might vary slightly. You wonder if maybe there is a threshold for this sort of thing – even in the average person. The threshold may depend upon an integrating factor, such as the one I've been talking about. If you could integrate things with a high degree of perfection, you might induce this telekinetic ability. That's an interesting idea.

We talk about having good and bad days and that a lot depends upon our mental attitude. Well, that's a very easy out. If you come up to something and say, 'I can climb this,' and you are totally convinced of it, as opposed to, 'I have my doubts whether I can climb it,' when it gets down to the line, how can you determine to what extent the difference in your performance is due to merely an improved attitude? Perhaps with an excellent mental attitude you not only integrate your moves better, but this in turn induces a telekinetic ability to levitate you slightly, even if it is only taking off a few ounces. A few ounces can make a tremendous difference. I have seen people go beyond their limits. We have a feeling for what someone's limits are, then we see him transcend them. We wonder if the individual isn't drawing upon some force that we are not aware of. Maybe you and I do the same thing at times, when our whole psyche is integrated sufficiently well. A goal or direction of climbing might be to attempt to research the activity and find out what needs to be done to cultivate such power, provided it can be shown to exist. I feel that the bond of friendship, the roped team, may be a manufacturer as well as a transmitter of psychic energy. It's interesting to speculate, isn't it?

The Direct North Overhang of the Scab in The Needles, early 1960s.

Gill at The Hagermeister Boulders, early '60s.

Gill climbing in The Shawangunks, New York, mid-60s.

Gill on Fatted Calf, Pueblo, Colorado, mid-70s.

Gill doing the one-finger pull-up, Fort Collins, Colorado, late 1960s.

Gill on Mental Block, Fort Collins, late '60s.

Gill along the Gem Lake Trail, near Estes Park, in the '60s.

Gill atop rock at Split Rocks, Colarado, in the '60s.

Gill, Bell Smith Springs, Southern Illinois, mid-60s.

Gill strolls an overhang at Veedauwoo, Wyoming, circa early 1960s.

John Gill, on Cutfinger Rock, early 1960s, Jenny Lake Boulders, Tetons.

Gill does a dynamic variation on Red Cross Rock, Jenny Lake boulders, Tetons, 1960s.

Pat Ament on one of Gill's bare granite routes, Gem Lake, above Estes Park, Colorado, circa 1968.

John Gill does Ament's "Milton" problem in Eldorado Canyon, late 1960s.

Gill climbing Eldorado Canyon, mid-60s.

John Gill considers an aesthetic variation, at Penny Ante Rock, Pueblo, circa 1978, photo by Pat Ament.

John Gill belays, in Little Owl Canyon, circa early 1980s, photo by Pat Ament.

Gill on his difficult Fatted Calf route, west of Pueblo, Colorado, static attempt, early 1980s.

About the Author

American rock climber and author Pat Ament is known for his creative writing, having published a range of impactful pieces such as his *Mountain* article 'The Black Canyon With Kor,' his imagistic masterpiece 'Swaramandal,' and his bestselling biographies *John Gill: Master of Rock* and Royal Robbins: *Spirit of the Age*. Much of his work has been praised for showing how humour and philosophy might fit into what is often particularly technical writing. In addition to this, dozens of his articles have appeared in anthologies of the best climbing and mountaineering writings due to their high quality. A keen gymnast whilst at university, Ament set free-climbing standards and partnered with masters including Layton Kor, Dave Rearick, Royal Robbins, Tom Higgins and Chuck Pratt. Ament became a bouldering inspiration and teamed with John Gill, achieving numerous first ascents both as a free-climber and a boulderer, throughout the 1960s and 1970s. His route *Supremacy Crack* in Colorado, in 1965, was one of the hardest short free climbs in the country, whilst his freeing of *Centre Route* on the Slack in 1967 was the first 5.11 in Yosemite. In September 2013 he was inducted into the Boulder Sports Hall of Fame, which celebrates and preserves the legacy of the city's greats who have excelled in their respective fields. Alongside these climbing successes, Ament has enjoyed recognition for his award-winning filmmaking, photography and art. Pat has won the Best Spirit Award at Telluride's Mountain film festival and, internationally, several outstanding achievement awards for film. Dubbed a 'Renaissance Man', Pat is a chess master, award-winning artist, pianist, songwriter, poet, photographer, and karate black belt. His humour, imagery, and gentle spirit have endeared him to a wide following.

Printed in the USA
CPSIA information can be obtained
at www.ICGtesting.com
JSHW012017140824
68134JS00025B/2465